THE PEREGRINE FUND
2017 ANNUAL REPORT

On our cover: Ollie is a young Milky Eagle-owl hand-raised as an education ambassador at our World Center for Birds of Prey. His gaze, skillfully captured by volunteer photographer Jim Shane, expresses the spirit of our *Vision 2050:* optimism, curiosity, and the belief that this is our time to shine.

Nearly thirty years ago I was given a challenge by The Peregrine Fund's first President, Bill Burnham—**save the Madagascar Fish Eagle.** To bring this incredible bird back from the brink of extinction we needed boots on the ground in this remote corner of the world to determine the nature of the problem and develop a conservation strategy to save this species. I was young and looking for a job, and Bill challenged me to raise the money to get this project off the ground. Within months I was awarded a grant and boarded a plane to Madagascar to work for one of the greatest conservation organizations on the planet. It was a gamble and a dream come true, but it was only the beginning.

Culturally and geographically, navigating Madagascar 30 years ago was much different than it is today. It was considered a wildly remote corner of the world, unaccustomed to Westerners and deeply dependent on unsustainable resource use. It became clear to me early on that this opportunity was much broader than developing a conservation, restoration, and management plan for the Madagascar Fish Eagle; it was about building relationships with local communities, listening to their needs, and supporting indigenous peoples in a way that honored their heritage and protected the habitats that all species relied on for survival.

The Madagascar Fish Eagle project was **the first successful community-based conservation effort in Madagascar—a game-changer in our field—**that's been successfully replicated by conservation organizations around the world.

Suffice it to say, this project was risky. But risk and tenacity are essential components for change that The Peregrine Fund has used time and time again to ensure the survival of birds of prey and the ecosystems on which they rely.

Thirty years later, The Peregrine Fund still believes in audacious goals. We do not shy away from tough problems, we face them head on, confident in our expertise and experience, and **driven by your generosity and belief that a better world is possible.**

THE PEREGRINE FUND

It was a gamble *and* a dream come true, but it was only the beginning.

Today we are rolling out a bold new plan for our future—*Vision 2050*— that draws on past lessons and successes and applies them to emerging and accelerating conservation problems faced by raptors and communities around the globe. Together we are:

- Launching a mobile app for data collection and web-based analysis tools to serve raptor biologists and connect their research around the world. The Global Raptor Impact Network (GRIN) will identify trends that *inform conservation action in real time.*

- Applying strategies developed in Madagascar to *save the Darien rainforest in Panama*—one of the most biodiverse places on the planet and one of the last strongholds of the magnificent Harpy Eagle in Central America. Peregrine Fund biologists are working on long-term economic solutions in partnership with the Emberá and Wounaan people, who have lived in the Darien for millennia, to help protect their native heritage and habitats.

- Developing public-private partnerships with landowners, state-level agencies and sporting groups across the western United States to encourage and incentivize the use of non-lead ammunition. We aim to *prevent lead poisoning,* the leading cause of death for California Condors.

- Preventing the death of endangered and critically endangered African vultures through the formation of Rapid Response to Poisoning Teams. These teams, made up of park rangers and government officials, are trained to identify a poisoning incident, collect evidence, and dispose of the poisoned carcass to *prevent further poisonings.*

You will find these new developments among the 22 high impact endeavors described in detail in the following pages. **Thank you** for playing such an important role in changing the future for nature and humanity. Your generous and ongoing support is creating a brighter future for us all.

With gratitude,

Richard T. Watson, Ph.D.
President and CEO

is ambitious, specific, unifying, inspirational, measurable, and—most importantly—empowering to the people and communities who bring it to life.

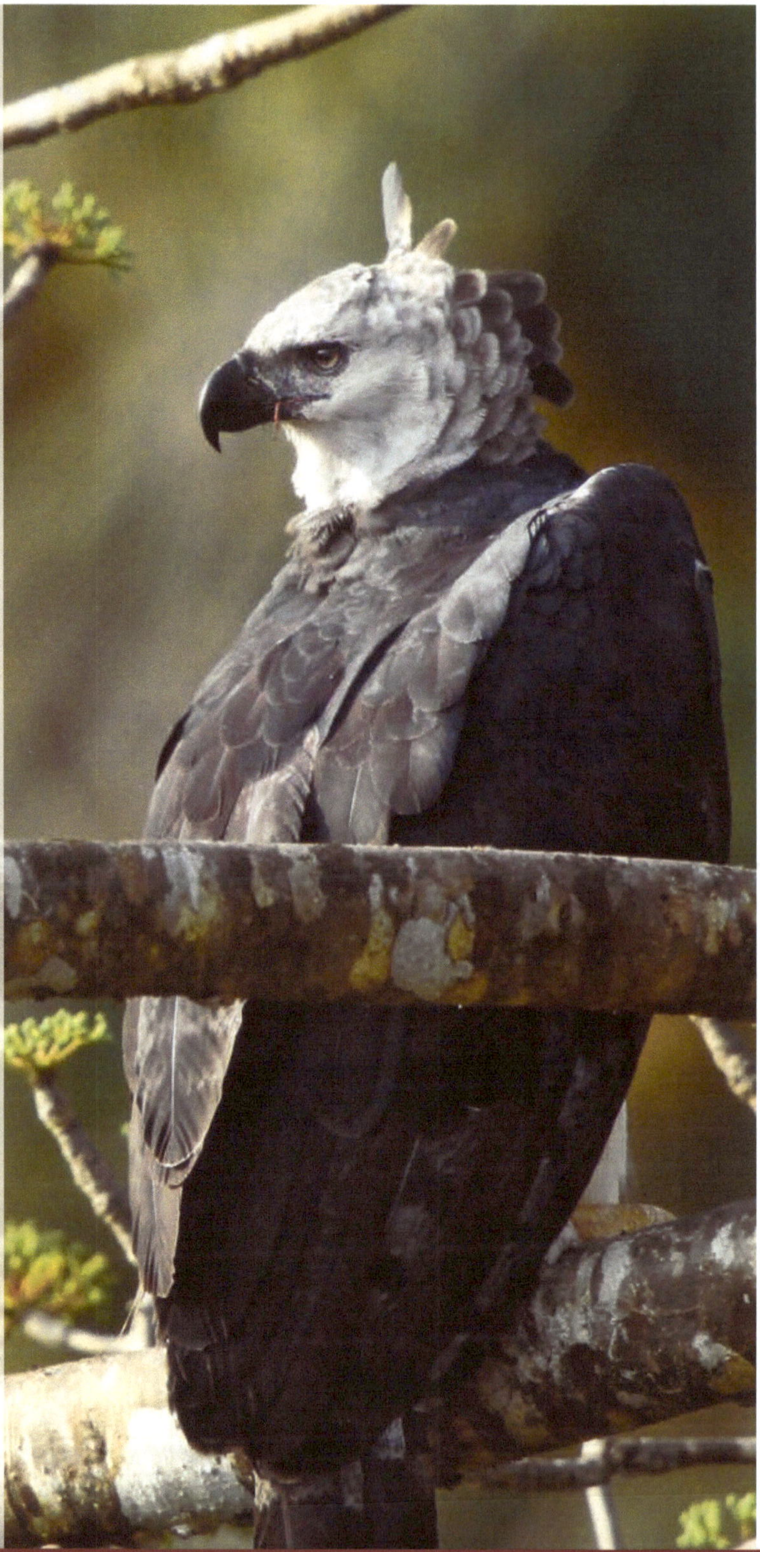

What does success look like?

Raptor populations and their environments thrive

Human communities are enriched by our work and raptors are valued by all.

We are the world leader for conserving birds of prey.

Our Core Values

We cherish birds of prey.

Sound scientific knowledge is our foundation.

We embrace diversity.

Integrity is precious and paramount.

Saving birds of prey is our life's work.

THE PEREGRINE FUND

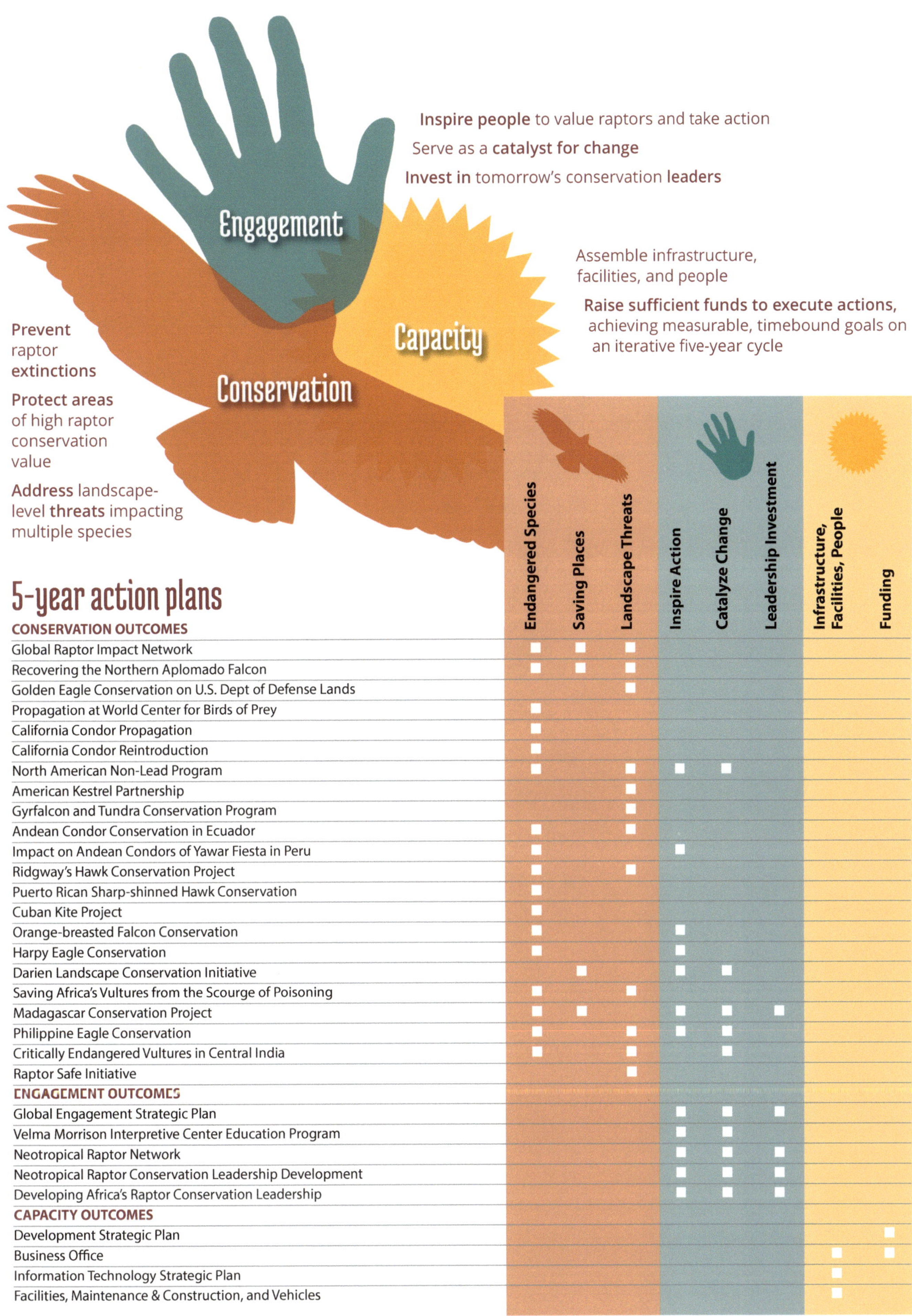

5-year action plans

	Endangered Species	Saving Places	Landscape Threats	Inspire Action	Catalyze Change	Leadership Investment	Infrastructure, Facilities, People	Funding
CONSERVATION OUTCOMES								
Global Raptor Impact Network	■	■	■					
Recovering the Northern Aplomado Falcon	■	■	■					
Golden Eagle Conservation on U.S. Dept of Defense Lands			■					
Propagation at World Center for Birds of Prey	■							
California Condor Propagation	■							
California Condor Reintroduction	■							
North American Non-Lead Program	■		■	■	■			
American Kestrel Partnership			■					
Gyrfalcon and Tundra Conservation Program			■					
Andean Condor Conservation in Ecuador	■		■					
Impact on Andean Condors of Yawar Fiesta in Peru	■			■				
Ridgway's Hawk Conservation Project	■		■					
Puerto Rican Sharp-shinned Hawk Conservation	■							
Cuban Kite Project	■							
Orange-breasted Falcon Conservation	■			■				
Harpy Eagle Conservation	■			■				
Darien Landscape Conservation Initiative		■		■	■			
Saving Africa's Vultures from the Scourge of Poisoning	■		■	■				
Madagascar Conservation Project	■	■		■	■	■		
Philippine Eagle Conservation	■		■	■	■			
Critically Endangered Vultures in Central India	■		■		■			
Raptor Safe Initiative			■					
ENGAGEMENT OUTCOMES								
Global Engagement Strategic Plan				■	■	■		
Velma Morrison Interpretive Center Education Program				■	■			
Neotropical Raptor Network				■	■	■		
Neotropical Raptor Conservation Leadership Development				■	■	■		
Developing Africa's Raptor Conservation Leadership				■	■	■		
CAPACITY OUTCOMES								
Development Strategic Plan								■
Business Office							■	■
Information Technology Strategic Plan							■	
Facilities, Maintenance & Construction, and Vehicles							■	

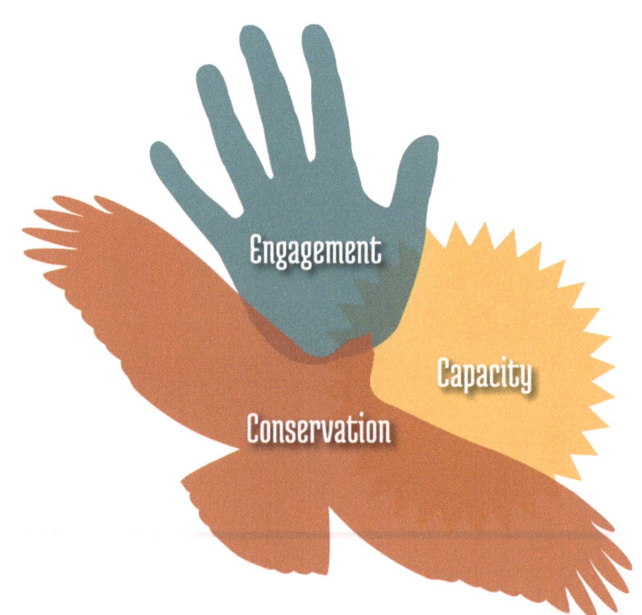

*Look for these icons on the following pages to see how each project fits as a strategic outcome of **Vision 2050**.*

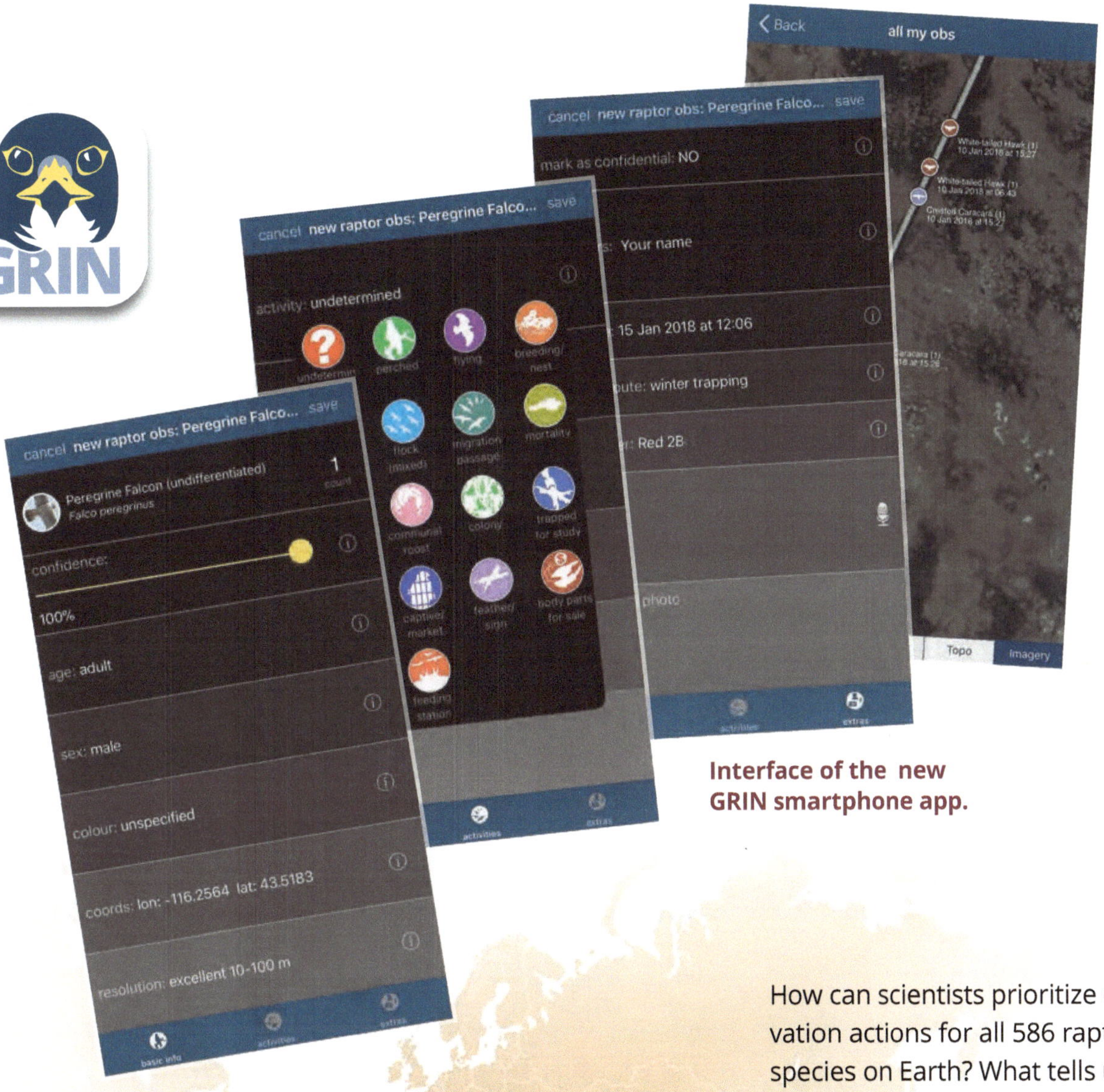

Interface of the new
GRIN smartphone app.

How can scientists prioritize conservation actions for all 586 raptor species on Earth? What tells us if a species is stable or endangered? The answers are complex, and even the world's most complete, up-to-date inventory of species is compiled from reports published years or even decades ago.

Eliminating that time lag could revolutionize conservation, setting a new pace for recognizing species declines...

CHANGE
to
THE
FUTURE

Critically endangered species don't have time to wait, especially those faced with rapidly growing threats like poison, electrocution, land development, and climate change. Accelerated threats must be met with accelerated tools to find and respond to populations in crisis.

Our new **Global Raptor Impact Network (GRIN)** will unify raptor data into a single, nimble network that is large enough to **identify threats and population trends in real time.**

We helped launched the African Raptor DataBank as a pilot program in collaboration with Habitat Info and other partners to collect data over a five-year period. More than 180,000 data points were collected via a smartphone app by dozens of scientific and conservation groups across the African continent. With this new information, a striking amount of lost habitat, hotspots of poisoning and electrocution, and sites with the best remaining habitat were mapped. **The result: six African vulture species were uplisted,** some to Critically Endangered status, on the Red List published by the International Union for the Conservation of Nature. Subsequent funding and attention to the plight of Africa's vultures increased significantly.

Based on the success of the African Raptor DataBank, we are now scaling it up for global use as GRIN. A beta version of the smartphone app was released to researchers at the 2017 Raptor Research Foundation conference, and developers plan to launch the new website in 2018. Besides serving as a collection point for new, real-time data, GRIN will house and safeguard historical data to provide a baseline for tracking population trends over long time periods.

Already, the data collected through GRIN is more comprehensive than any data set currently existing for raptors, and includes first-time global data sets on lifespan, productivity, diet, and habitat. We can accurately map the range, demography, and behaviors of raptor species and identify trends quickly.

The ability to recognize trends across a broad landscape or a set of species is especially valuable. For example, the catastrophic decline in Asian vulture populations was difficult to quantify with the data-gathering systems of the 1990s. If a similar catastrophe occurs now, GRIN will enable us to quickly assess the trend and sound the alarm.

Hunters and anglers often have the deepest and most respected voices within the chorus of support for wildlife in North America. Showing pride in their heritage— protecting the delicate balance of predators, prey, and scavengers—sportsmen and women contribute more than a billion dollars each year toward conservation.

When wildlife is under threat, hunters are among the first to notice and act. That's why we're alerting them to a safer choice of ammunition...

Hunters are heroes for scavenging animals, particularly in winter when a gut pile or carcass can prevent starvation. Unfortunately, the smallest trace of lead ammunition in that valuable food source causes unintended side effects. Unlike monolithic solids such as all-copper bullets, lead bullets scatter into microscopic fragments. Scientific evidence from numerous sources shows that lead-tainted meat is by far the primary source of lead poisoning in wildlife. An animal that eats lead is sickened and can die slowly from failure of the central nervous system—certainly not the aim of an informed, ethical shooter.

Lead was routinely included in paint, fuel, and even food prior to medical discoveries in the last century. And as residents of Flint, Michigan, can attest, ending exposure to this preventable threat is a major undertaking with high stakes—protecting the health of our most vulnerable. Those vulnerable residents include raptors like eagles and vultures whenever remains of shot animals are left in the wild. **Even the mighty California Condor, with its nine-foot wingspan, can die after eating lead from ammunition residues.**

Copper ammunition (left) does not fragment like lead-based ammunition.

The North American Non-Lead Partnership is committed to working with hunters to end lead poisoning of wildlife by increasing the use of non-lead ammunition. The hunting community took steps in 1991 to manage the use of lead shot for waterfowl, with positive results for Bald Eagles and game animals alike. To expand on that protective effect, we're asking shooters for a simple, voluntary fix: switch to non-lead ammunition for instances where meat or a gutpile might be left for wild animals to scavenge.

In addition to advocating for this voluntary switch, the partnership supports ongoing research about lead exposure pathways. Sound science is one of the pillars of American hunters' conservation ethic, and the partnership's roots are in long-established, well-respected scientific organizations.

The partnership does not seek to ban lead ammunition, firearms, or hunting. Its singular focus is safeguarding wildlife—an achievable goal with the help of hunters, America's first conservationists.

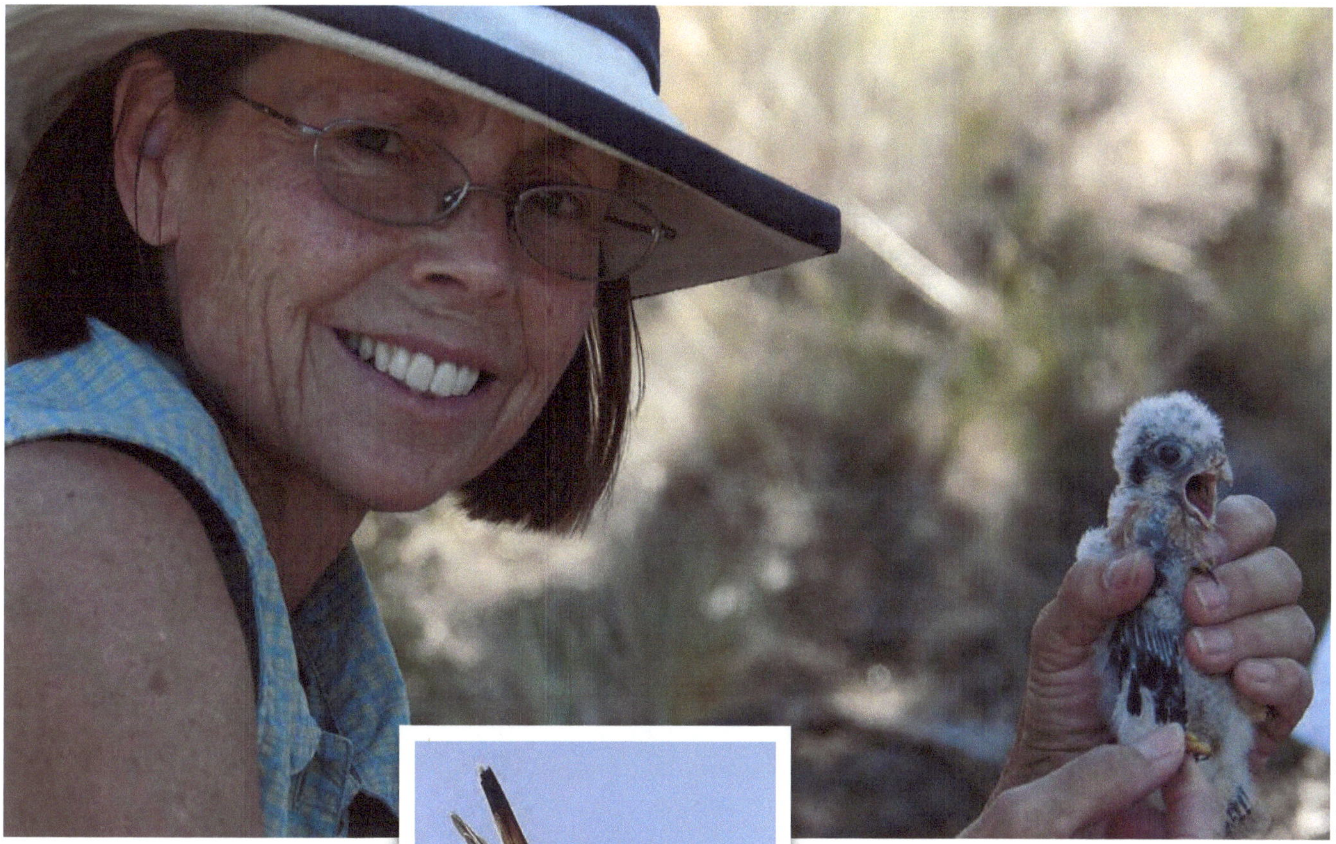

Kevin Smith

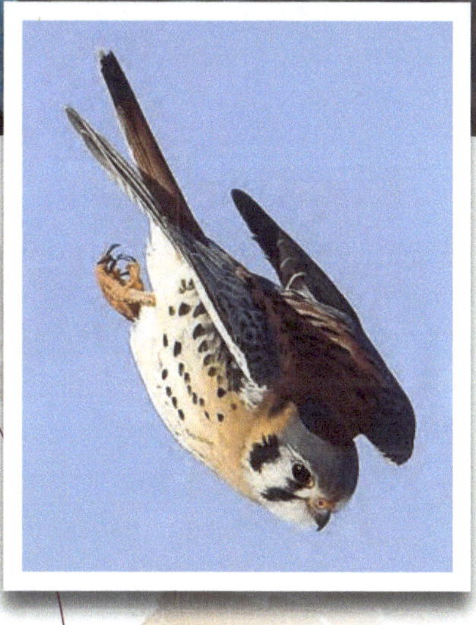

Rob Palmer

American Kestrels are North America's most plentiful falcon, guarding cityscape ledges or hovering over rural roadsides to hunt rodents and insects. This small falcon is familiar even to casual observers, but a look at population levels reveals a perplexing mystery: continent-wide, kestrels have declined by nearly half since the 1960s.

Researchers have yet to find the definitive threat—or threats—that are making this "common" species uncommon. As the global specialist for birds of prey, we have united researchers to develop the "big picture" before it's too late...

The American Kestrel ranges from the Yukon to Tierra del Fuego, so compiling a "snapshot" of kestrel life requires a veritable army of observers. Fortunately, kestrels are cavity-nesters and readily inhabit nest boxes during the breeding season, making observation relatively simple so that virtually anyone can contribute data to our continent-wide study. "Citizen scientists" are the eyes, ears, and hearts of the American Kestrel Partnership, contributing countless hours and enthusiasm and creating an international community throughout the Americas to unite people based on love for their backyard falcon.

Although many local nest box programs exist, the American Kestrel Partnership is the only coordinator of an international network of professional and citizen scientists, managing a single database to look for far-reaching trends that could explain population declines.

Jim Shane

Now with five years of data, we have narrowed our inquiry to go beyond simple "head counts" and delve into questions about the kestrel's life cycle. Are adults returning after winter to breed? Are they dying at high rates during breeding, migration, or over-wintering? Are they breeding less often, or failing when they do breed? And, critically, how are they affected by land use, contaminants, climate, predators, and other species? To find answers, our colleagues at Boise State University and UCLA are conducting genetic analyses using feather samples gathered by our partners throughout North and South America.

We've also discovered that in nest box studies, just as in real estate, location is key. Nest boxes are not the "golden ticket" to halting population declines, and could even harm wildlife if placed incorrectly. These findings reinforce our focus on responsible nest box place-ment and standardized, consistent monitoring to ensure that American Kestrel boxes are placed in safe locations.

USGS Breeding Bird Survey data

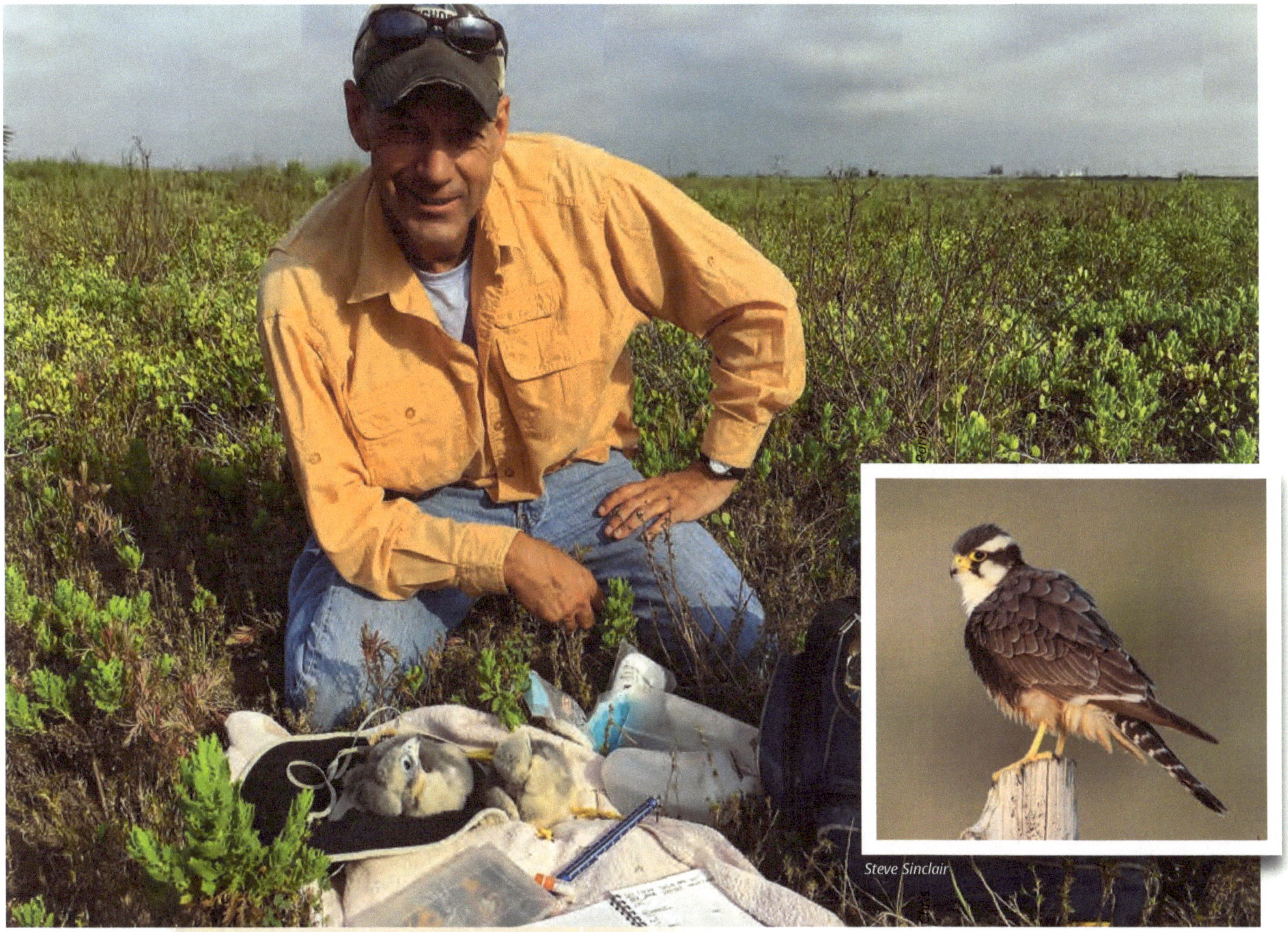

Steve Sinclair

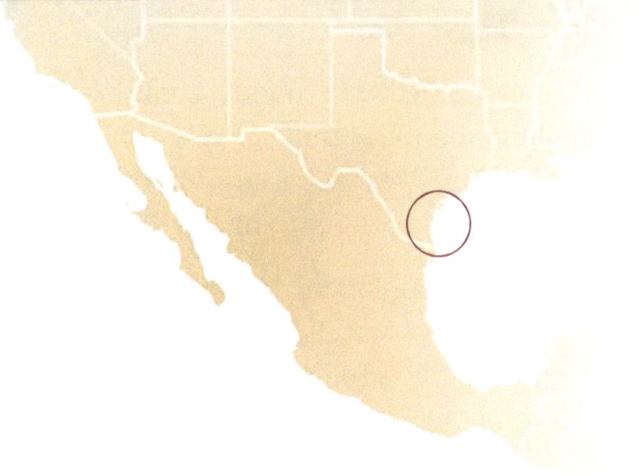

After an absence of at least forty years, a stable Aplomado Falcon population thrives along the Gulf Coast thanks to our breeding and release program, in partnership with landowners and collaborators. So why is this falcon still on the U.S. Endangered Species List?

The wild population has yet to exceed the recommended threshold of 60 pairs. We found the root problem, then adapted our strategy...

Unlike Peregrine Falcons that range across a variety of habitats, Aplomado Falcons depend on wide-open grasslands with mature yucca plants for nesting, ample migrating birds as prey, and a balance of other predators. Intact grasslands had become so scarce that in 2013 **we stopped breeding and releasing Aplomado Falcons and focused our efforts on finding and nurturing habitat.**

Overgrown brush is an enemy of healthy grasslands because it crowds out yucca, the falcons' preferred nesting plants, and harbors predators like Great Horned Owls. Brush removal is difficult and expensive, but the benefits for falcons and other species are significant. We now advise agencies on grassland restoration and are seeking private landowners who can commit to the same actions. Our priority is restoring areas with recently-abandoned Aplomado territories, or occupied territories where brush is beginning to encroach.

To offset a lack of yucca plants, we erected dozens of barred nesting platforms. Pairs using them raise as many young as pairs in yucca nests, and twice as many as pairs nesting on brush or the ground!

Dave Allen, allenwildlife.com

Our advanced computer analysis, the "Aplo-model," confirms that **our approach is working: reproduction along the Texas Gulf coast is ample to sustain a growing population in suitable habitat.** With a current total of 39 breeding pairs, the Aplomado Falcon is well on its way to reaching the de-listing goal of 60.

How will we continue to grow the population? **Expanding habitat is key.** Although the Aplomado is a medium-sized falcon, it requires a relatively large area to nest and raise young. Roughly a third of the population and its habitat still lacks formal protection, and rapid development in the Lower Rio Grande Valley could pose a threat. Fortunately, we've spent decades stitching together a patchwork of private lands, public parks, and wildlife refuges. So far we have enrolled 2.25 million acres within the falcon's historical range, with a fraction currently suitable for Aplomado Falcons.

Next year we will gather partners to share the latest knowledge and refine this species' recovery plan, which was first drafted in 1990.

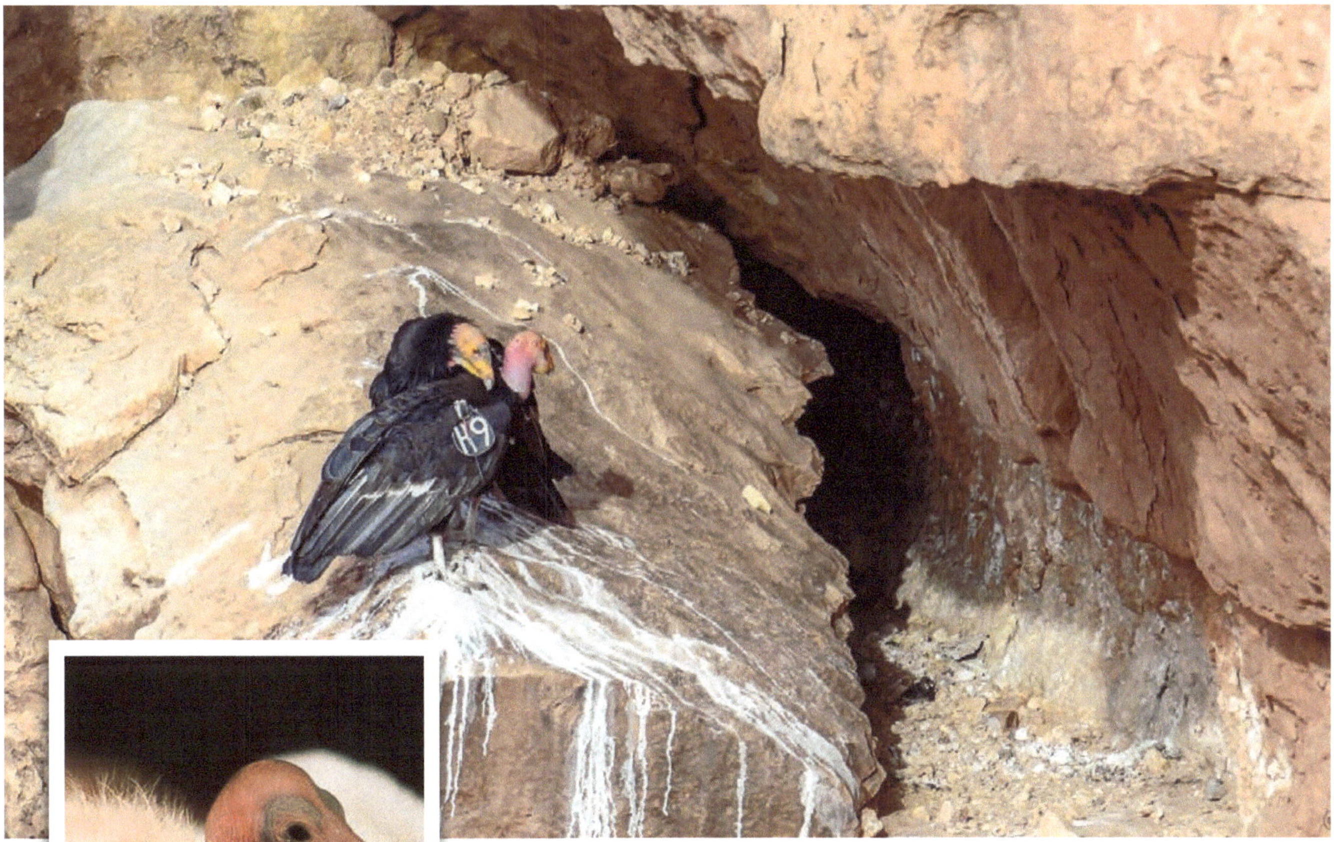

Alan Clampitt

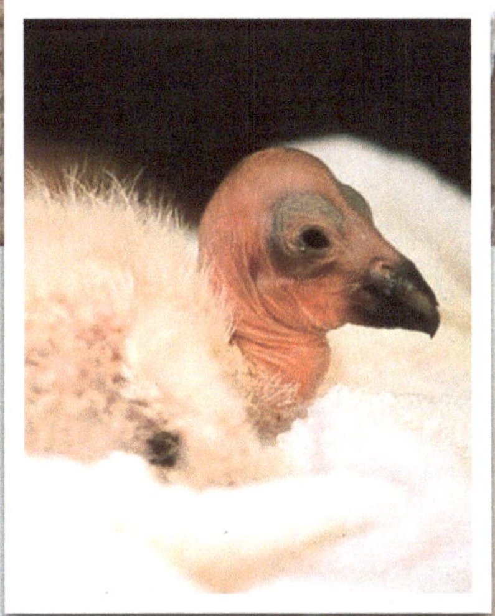

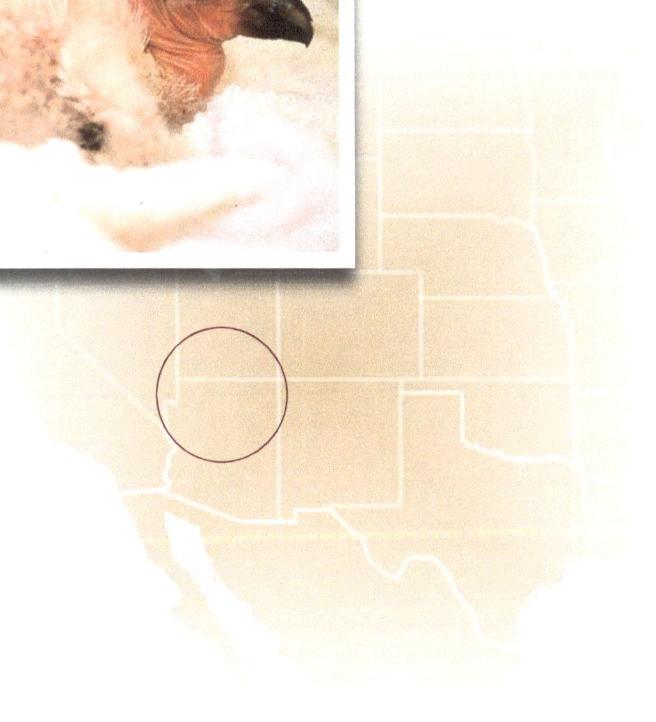

Long before humans arrived in North America, these finely tuned scavengers relied in part on hunters—sabertooth cats and other large predators—for carrion. Condors' clean-up role hasn't changed, but new hunters to the scene can unintentionally leave behind a deadly contaminant: lead from spent ammunition.

Despite our efforts to recover this critically endangered species through captive breeding, release, and monitoring, preventable lead poisoning stands in the way. But like these giants of the sky, we're learning to rely on hunters...

Our California Condor breeding program began in 1996 at our facility in Boise, Idaho. Young condors are transported to release sites in Arizona, California, and Baja, Mexico.

We have re-established a free-flying population that now numbers 82 condors ranging from the Grand Canyon north into Utah. We annually test every condor we can trap. Last season, 87% tested positive for lead exposure, and we treated 33 condors for extremely high lead. Two did not survive.

Twelve pairs in the Arizona-Utah flock showed breeding behavior this year, and nine laid eggs. Four hatched chicks, and three of the chicks survived.

The public can see the first free flights of captive-bred juveniles from our Vermilion Cliffs release site each September. Year-round, our Condor Cliffs exhibit in Boise, Idaho, offers a closer look at these impressive birds.

1/2018

The California Condor is a hardy species that survived mass extinctions of the last Ice Age, yet **the entire population was reduced to just 22 individuals** by the 1980s. Scientists suspected that lead poisoning played a role in the species' decline, and recent research by The Peregrine Fund confirmed that over half of all condor deaths are due to this one preventable cause. The 'aha' moment occurred when we x-rayed deer harvested with common lead-based bullets. A constellation of tiny fragments, too numerous to count, appear in the tissue surrounding the bullet's path. Not only do California Condors ingest this lead, it's evident that many other species, even humans, may be exposed to lead-tainted meat. Like the canary in the coal mine, the California Condor has alerted us to an unforeseen and preventable hazard.

Chris Parish

By switching to non-lead ammunition, **hunters can eliminate the potential for lead exposure to any animal.** Thanks to our work with Arizona and Utah wildlife agencies over the last decade, more than 80% of deer hunters on Arizona's Kaibab Plateau now take voluntary actions to prevent exposure. Their conservation ethic will inspire others to make the switch to copper, but we need to spread the message to a wider audience.

To accomplish this, we are uniting to form a **North American Non-Lead Partnership,** whose sole purpose is to reach hunters, shooters, and other sporting and conservation groups with information about preventing lead poisoning.

The world population of California Condors continues to grow slowly, with **446 now in existence.** More than half live in the wilderness, ready to fill their niche as skilled scavengers if only we can make their world a little safer.

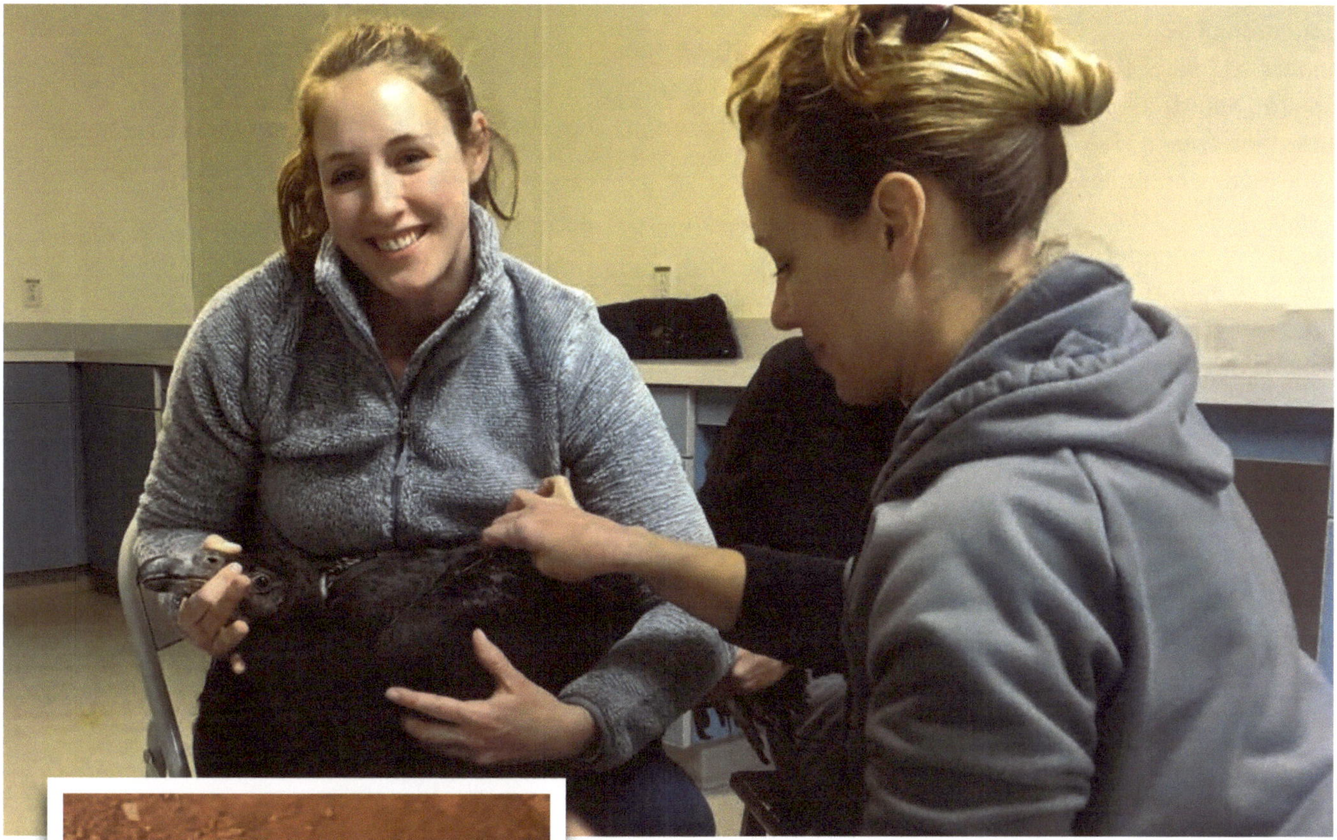

Hana Weaver

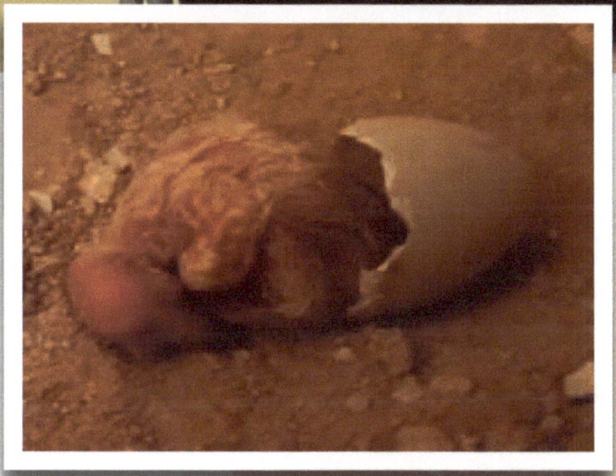

Marti Jenkins

By the time most California Condors mature to reproductive age at about six years, they have encountered a wealth of dangers in the wild. Surviving predators, accidents, and toxins is no guarantee of breeding success though—condors' first nesting attempts often fail before the chick is old enough to leave its nest cave, and chicks that do fledge depend on their parents for a year or more. Usually, a condor pair in the wild raises a single offspring every other year.

Nature has set the stage for condor populations to grow very slowly, so our breeding program is essential...

THE PEREGRINE FUND

California Condors would almost certainly be extinct if not for breeding programs, which started in the 1980s with the last 22 condors removed from the wild. The Peregrine Fund was invited by the U.S. Fish and Wildlife Service to breed condors at its World Center for Birds of Prey in Boise, Idaho, beginning in 1993. We work closely with partners coordinated by the U.S. Fish and Wildlife Service, including the three zoos that breed condors (Los Angeles, San Diego, and Oregon). Together we set annual goals for the number of condors to be produced, and designate where the previous year's chicks should be released.

By controlling risks like predators, accidents, and food contamination, we enable our captive breeders to consistently achieve success rates above 90 percent. More than half of all California Condors raised in breeding programs, 16–20 young each year, come from our facility in Boise and are divided among several release sites, including the one we manage near the Grand Canyon.

Our propagation specialists are experienced field biologists with a keen awareness of condor behavior and social structure. They create conditions that not only keep condor parents secure and content, but also prepare the young hatchlings to become wild survivors.

Because condors are highly intelligent and curious, they can rapidly learn to associate humans with food rewards. This can spell disaster for a condor, especially one destined to fly free near a high-tourist area like the Grand Canyon. To keep our young condors from becoming familiar with humans, we design their enclosures so they rarely see or hear people. We even employ a small herd of goats to clear nearby brush rather than using mowers!

Thanks to the success of condor breeding programs, four of the original 22 are so well-represented in the wild population's genetics that they are no longer needed for breeding. **Those hardy, long-lived birds returned to the wild homes they inhabited forty years ago to live their remaining years with hundreds of free-flying descendants—no longer the "last" of their kind.**

Paul Spurling

Jeannie Konkel

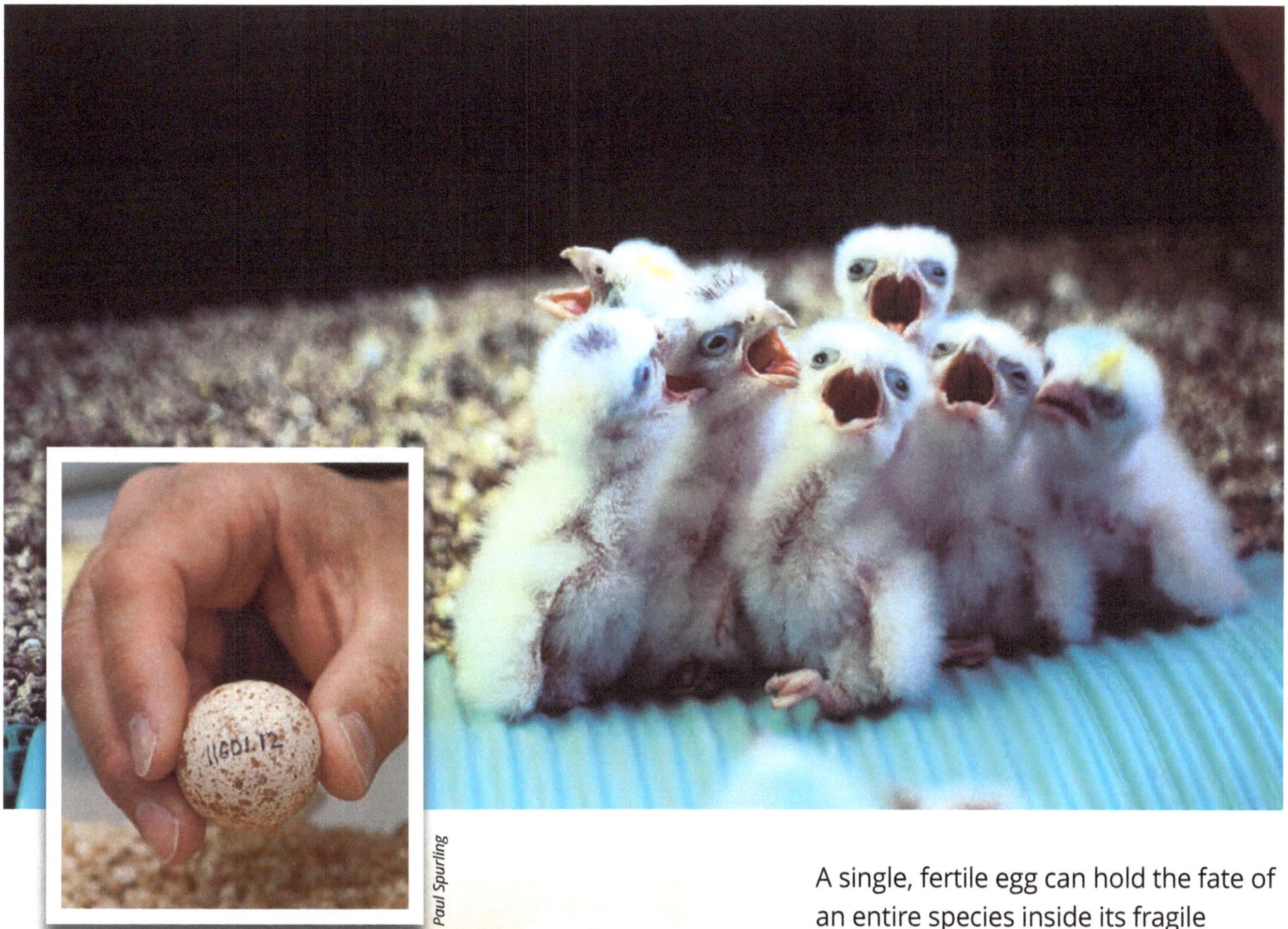

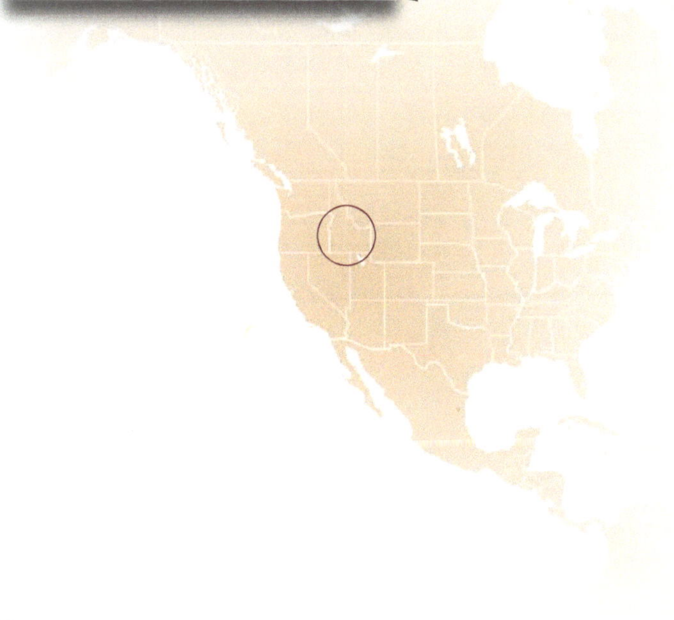

A single, fertile egg can hold the fate of an entire species inside its fragile shell— a fact woefully apparent to our founders as they struggled almost 50 years ago to coax a viable egg from the Peregrine Falcons entrusted to them. Even more rare and precious were the tiny eggs laid by the last four Mauritius Kestrels in our care a few years later.

Those early experiences led to breakthroughs in biology and species recovery, and they also laid the foundation for **The Peregrine Fund: raptor breeding experts and, more importantly, dedicated people who find a way no matter how daunting...**

Since hatching our first Peregrine Falcon in 1973, we have served as the global expert in captive propagation of endangered birds of prey. **Those last four Mauritius Kestrels were the forebears of a now-thriving population, and the lessons we learned have been handed down as well.** Altogether our staff has reared more than 3,000 Peregrine Falcons, 2,000 Northern Aplomado Falcons, and 250 California Condors—plus 18 other species from Harpy Eagles to American Kestrels. Today we manage the world's largest captive population of California Condors, the most endangered bird in North America.

Kate Davis

Our methods are widely published, and have in fact enabled others to breed birds of prey around the world, both for falconry and for scientific and conservation pursuits. No other organization, however, has the facilities and experience to breed a variety of raptors at a similar scale—a scale that could be called upon if a raptor species suffers catastrophic decline. As threats to birds of prey increase across the globe, we are constantly refining our skills in case extreme measures are needed to prevent extinction.

Conservation breeding is not always the best solution, however; it requires careful laboratory controls, round-the-clock staff, transportation of young birds to wild release sites, and field attendants to support young birds as they learn to hunt and defend themselves—all at a heavy financial cost that may not show positive results for years.

For some species, early intervention can curtail the need for intensive conservation breeding. In the Dominican Republic we perfected a new technique of relocating young Ridgway's Hawks from their parents' nests to a safer territory before they learn to fly. This "assisted dispersal" approach has resulted in an entirely new, self-sustaining population of hawks, buying us time to address the threats that had reduced their numbers, like human persecution and habitat loss.

Roy Toft

David Anderson

The Gyrfalcon is a raptor of extremes: not only is it the largest falcon on Earth, it's also one of the few animals adapted to harsh Arctic winters. Unfortunately, it is also considered the North American bird species most vulnerable to climate change.

Like polar bears and harp seals, Gyrfalcons can only survive in cold climates. Against a backdrop of shifting prey availability, fluctuating weather, and competition from other species moving northward, the Gyrfalcon's survival is uncertain. **Knowing that intervention may be necessary someday, we are learning all we can now...**

THE PEREGRINE FUND

Fascination with Gyrfalcons is deeply rooted in The Peregrine Fund's history: Tom Cade, our founder, was among the first to publish research about them. Later, our long-term studies in Greenland revealed new information about the species. As climate change concerns began to mount, we already had the unique expertise, partnerships, and data to address the unknown. We hosted an international conference in 2011, then convened the Tundra Conservation Network to connect partners from all eight Arctic countries and multiple disciplines.

Roy Toft

Collaboration is vital for saving this species, which has been studied in isolated pockets for centuries thanks in part to the Gyrfalcon's popularity with falconers. We launched the Polar Raptor Databank in 2017 to collect historical and new data in a secure repository, and concurrently published *Applied Raptor Ecology,* a manual that sets standards for gathering comparable, high-quality data. From anywhere in the world, researchers can now record unlimited observations and access real-time analysis tools. As data are accumulated and shared, ecologists can then answer questions about global population trends and identify factors that have the greatest impact on Arctic raptors.

Our fieldwork is contributing surprising findings to this body of work using motion-activated cameras at Gyrfalcon nests on Alaska's Seward Peninsula. Observing prey items in the photos, we have found that Gyrfalcons rely heavily on ptarmigan, but also adapt their diet when ptarmigan numbers decrease. Cameras documented one female Gyrfalcon moving her young out of a falling nest and carrying it to a new location. We also met some "visitors" to the nests, including grizzly bear, red fox, wolverine, and ravens.

Our fieldwork will continue long-term, as will collaboration with researchers worldwide who are invited to a Symposium on Arctic Raptors at our headquarters in 2020. Ultimately, we will synthesize all shared knowledge about Gyrfalcons into an adaptive management plan to energize conservation action around the world. Acting on sound science, together we will be the difference between survival and extinction for this icon of the Arctic.

Sebastian Kohn

Harold Stiver

With its more than 10-foot wingspan, a soaring Andean Condor is truly magnificent. The ancients depicted it in art more than 4,000 years ago, and five modern countries revere it as a national symbol. But despite its cherished status, this majestic New World Vulture species is declining throughout its vast range from Colombia to Tierra del Fuego, and the northernmost populations are Critically Endangered.

Like other Vultures around the world, Andean Condors are often at odds with changes in human customs. Our research is pointing out ways...

THE PEREGRINE FUND

Several thousand Andean Condors were reported in Ecuador a century ago, but today we know of just 100. **Fortunately, our efforts show that it's not too late:**

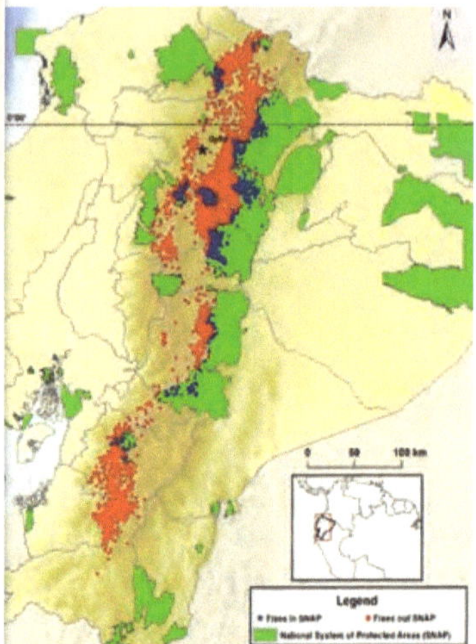

since 2012 we've found 14 nests, compared to the single nest that had been monitored prior to our study. We gained a wealth of data (left) from nine telemetry-tagged birds, which will help justify immediate conservation measures. Of 31 condors whose blood we tested, all were in good health. And we learned that inbreeding has not occurred, thanks to gene flow between two sub-populations.

The most significant threats are from ranchers who shoot or poison condors in the belief that the birds attack cattle. Although hungry condors have been known to occasionally kill young calves, our studies show they prefer carrion if it's available. Competition for carrion is stiff, however, because of feral and free-roaming dogs. Lead exposure may be another threat; we found high levels in condors from Argentina.

These factors are compounded by the species' naturally slow reproductive rates. Andean Condors need at least seven years to mature before they mate, after which successful pairs only raise a single chick every other year. Productivity can't keep pace with mortality, making the population extremely vulnerable.

Hernan Vargas

The Andean Condor has advantages that bode well for its recovery. Residents and tourists in South America are genuinely interested in saving this cultural treasure, and we've reached millions in documentaries and with a new Spanish-language website (investigacioncondorecuador.com). We partner with Ecuador's Ministry of Environment, and lead the Andean Condor Conservation Network, a continent-wide research consortium.

In time, we hope to preserve habitat for the Andean Condor that will also protect key watersheds and maintain the biodiversity of the Amazon Basin, fulfilling this species' ancient role in Andean myth as a symbol of health and immortality.

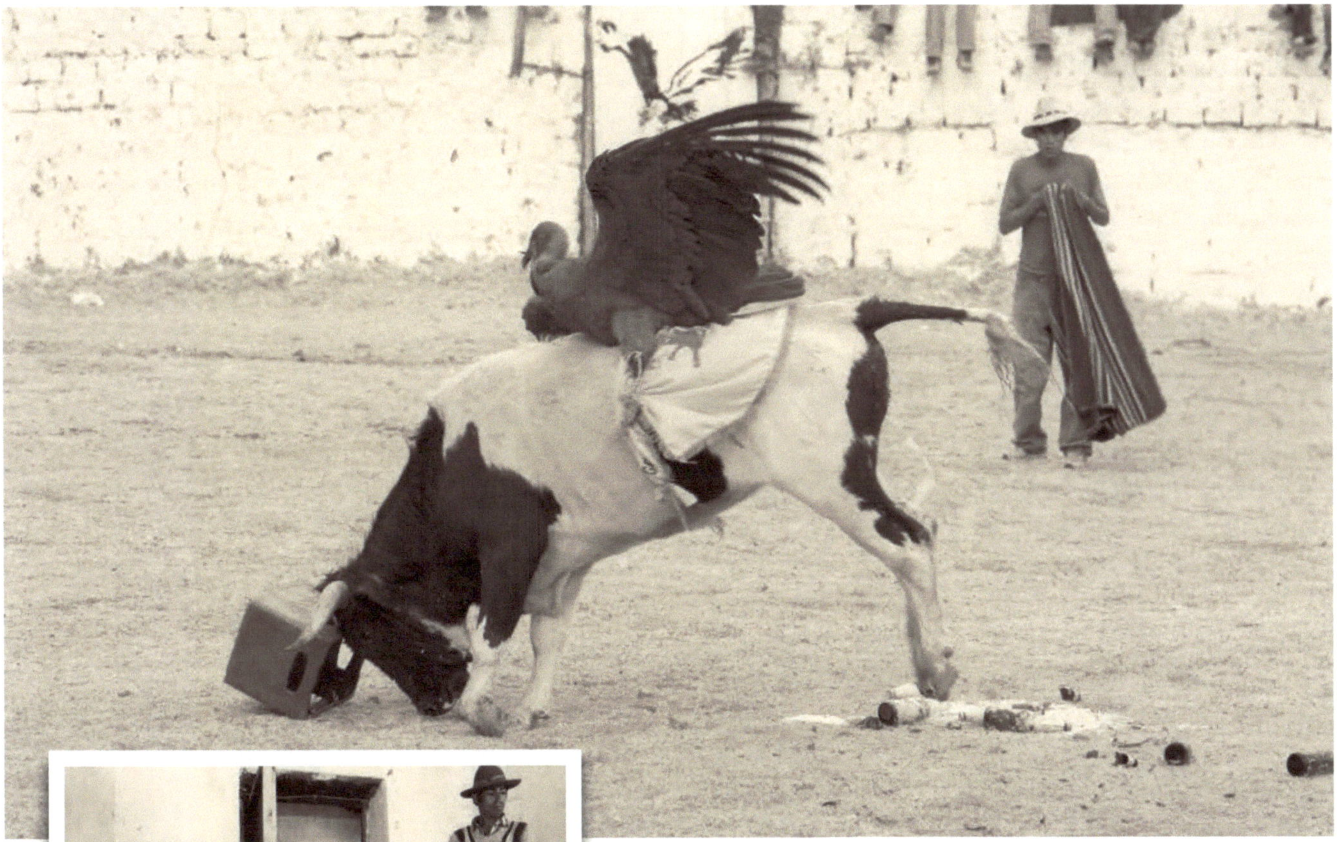

Cecilia Larrabure

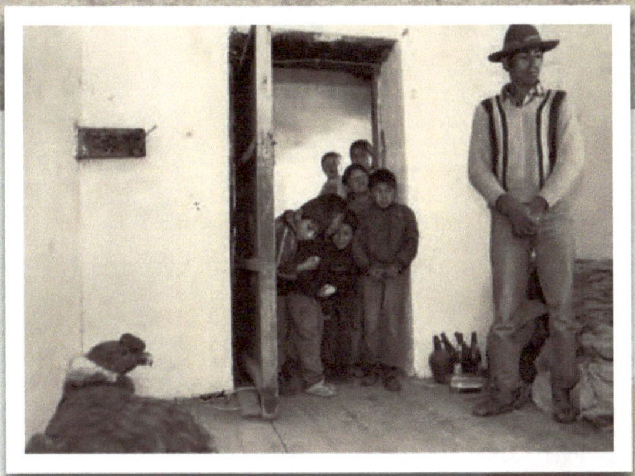

Cecilia Larrabure

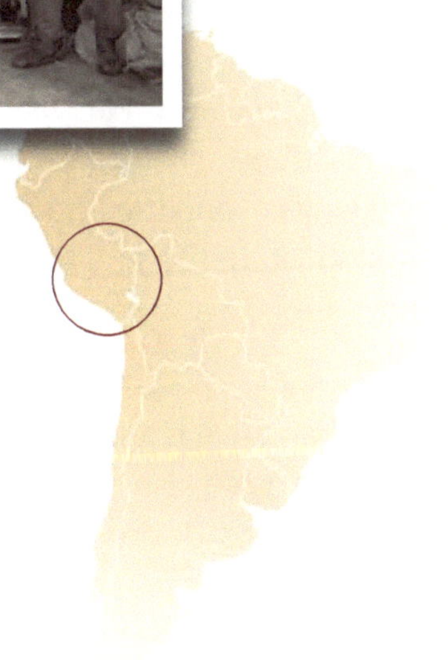

Every July, villagers in southern Peru celebrate independence from Spanish colonial rule. Known as Yawar Fiesta or "Blood Festival," the event attracts tourists to witness a life-or-death struggle: a wild Andean Condor, symbolizing the Inca people, is tied on the back of a bull representing Spain. A matador then goads the two frightened animals into a bloody fight.

Andean Condors are already in steep decline. This long-lived bird, an icon of Peru's cultural heritage, urgently needs protection...

THE PEREGRINE FUND

We partner with Centro de Ornitología y Biodiversidad (CORBIDI) and the Peruvian Forest Service (SERFOR), both of whom are committed to eliminating the negative impacts of Yawar Fiestas on Andean Condors.

In 2018 we hope to provide grants to two students and recruit volunteers to find, document, and film Yawar Fiestas, trapping locations, and treatment of the condors. Footage will be used to create short documentaries.

Our plans include conducting a pilot program in three communities, providing teacher training and educational materials for students of all ages. Our message will focus on the importance of condors in Andean culture and folklore, as well as protection of the species.

We'll engage local leaders as well, and train police to safely deliver injured Andean Condors to authorized rehabilitation centers.

01/2018

We don't yet know how many villages hold Yawar Fiestas, but current estimates suggest that 60 wild Andean Condors are trapped every year for the spectacles. The birds are typically kept in unsafe conditions for several days, paraded through the streets, and fed alcohol before the main event. Those that live through the ordeal are released, but it's unknown whether they survive or for how long.

Although Peruvian law forbids the capture of wild animals, the festivals are carried out under the leadership of local mayors, police, and priests. Peruvians revere the Andean Condor as sacred, symbolizing a god descending from the heavens to fight in their behalf. **Most are not aware that the ritual harms or kills the condors.** And with the enticement of tourist money, we believe the number of communities hosting Yawar Fiestas is growing.

Cecilia Larrabure

Our data from Ecuador and elsewhere shows Andean Condors already in decline, poisoned or shot primarily by ranchers in retaliation for livestock deaths. (Although condors feed mostly on carrion, they are able to occasionally kill calves.) **Since Andean Condors only raise a single chick every other year, losses related to Yawar Fiestas are simply not sustainable.** Condors fly vast distances, and it's likely that the toll from Yawar Fiestas affects the entire population, which ranges from Colombia to Tierra del Fuego. Our immediate task is to determine how many festivals take place, and the impact they have on the species as a whole. Our partners, staff, students, and volunteers are poised to do the necessary fact-finding in July of this year by attending numerous fiestas to observe, document, and film.

With this information in hand, we hope to influence local officials and train them to protect Andean Condors. We'll also design and launch an outreach program this year appealing to Peruvians' desire to protect their cultural heritage and respect condors, while offering a new perspective about the species' precarious existence. We'll conduct a pilot program in three communities, evaluate the effectiveness, then adjust as needed and expand throughout the region until we achieve **our goal: ending the trapping of Andean Condors for Yawar Fiestas.**

www.peregrinefund.org • 208|362-3716   Contact Geoff Pampush: 406|388-7717 • gpampush@peregrinefund.org

Jose Vargas

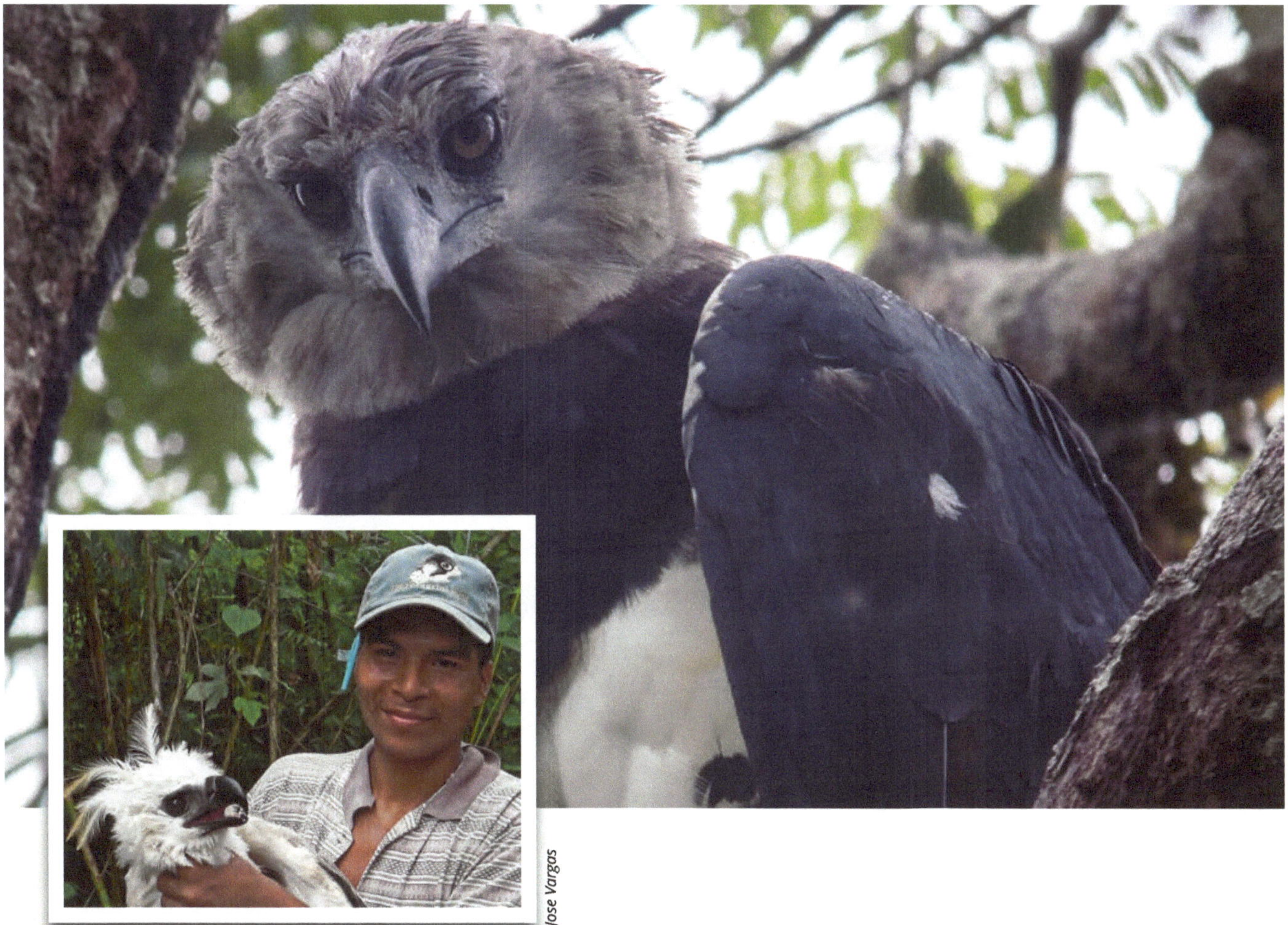

David L. Anderson

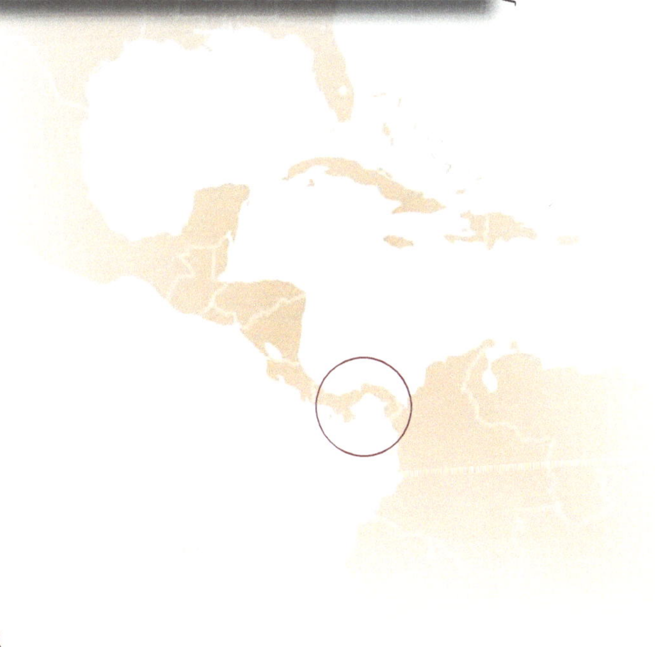

With their long, curved beaks and talons the size of grizzly bear claws, Harpy Eagles are among the largest and most powerful eagles in the world. These commanding birds swoop through the rain forests of Latin America, routinely picking up prey weighing more than 15 pounds—and sometimes equal to their own weight.

As Panama's national bird, the Harpy Eagle is a "flagship" species—an emblem of a fragile ecosystem whose fate depends on us...

01/2018

Harpy Eagle mortality
Human-caused: 46%
Natural: 54%

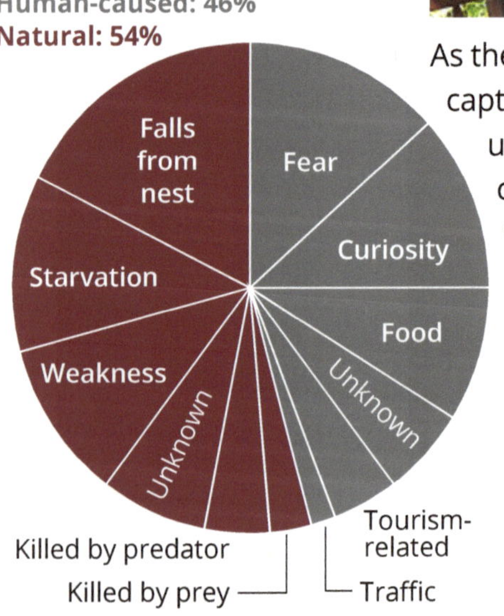

Although Harpy Eagles maintain healthy populations in South America, **the outlook is troubling in Central America, where in most countries they are listed as Critically Endangered.** New roads, mining, slash-and-burn farming, and forest fires threaten to destroy intact rain forests that are crucial to their survival.

The greatest concentration of Harpy Eagles in Central America can be found in Darien Province, Panama, where The Peregrine Fund has been working since 2000 on one of the longest projects ever conducted for the species. Our insights into breeding, dispersal, habitat, diet, and causes of mortality are pivotal in mapping the future of this long-lived, charismatic eagle.

We haven't worked alone, though—for 17 years we have partnered with local communities in our Darien work. Every year we train Emberá and Wounaan technicians and volunteers who not only conduct field work and help us mount transmitters (below), but also spread the word within their communities about the value of Harpy Eagles. Emberá and Wounaan people have inhabited the Darien for time immemorial, and their ability to manage development from outside forces is essential to preserving their homeland along with the eagles' habitat. Our support for the people of Darien is crucial, and assisting with sustainable jobs and education is an integral part of our conservation approach.

David L. Anderson

As the first organization to ever establish a program to breed Harpy Eagles in captivity and release them to the wild, our familiarity with the species is unmatched. But we have more to learn to conserve the Harpy Eagle in the chaotic years ahead. We need to understand the degree to which various types of human disturbances affect the eagles' ability to hunt, establish territories, and reproduce. If factors like habitat fragmentation, tourism, agriculture, and road building limit the population size, **we must have solid data to advocate effectively for preserving this high-demand landscape.**

Our newly-launched Darien Conservation Initiative, which aims to preserve four million acres of rain forests in Panama, is firmly grounded on the relationships we've cultivated for nearly two decades of studying and conserving Harpy Eagles.

Saving Rain Forest for Humans and Harpy Eagles

Darien Conservation Initiative

David L. Anderson

Deep in the innermost reaches of Panama, on the border with Colombia, lies the Darien Gap—the largest and wildest remaining stretch of rain forest north of the Amazon. Indigenous peoples have lived traditionally in the area for millennia, and the largest population of Harpy Eagles in Central America nests in the forest's towering native trees.

Situated on the bridge between North and South America, the Darien and its inhabitants are at geographic and historic crossroads. **By blending their traditional values with sustainable modern livelihoods we will empower them...**

The Darien region is home to 54 raptor species as well as jaguars, tapirs, ocelots, and critically-endangered cotton-top tamarins. With a fifth of its plants found nowhere else and thousands of plant and animal species to be discovered, **Darien is one of the most biologically rich places on earth—a biodiversity "hotspot."**

We have studied the threatened Harpy Eagle in Darien since 2000, when we also established Panama's first non-governmental organization for raptor conservation. For many years, we also raised and released Harpy Eagles and conducted public education and outreach in Panama, and our studies on wild populations are ongoing. Our friends throughout the country provide us an intimate understanding of the complex pressures on the Darien and its inhabitants. Now, we are prepared—together—to meet an accelerating threat: land development.

As decades-long civil conflict in neighboring Colombia comes to a peaceful end, forces are organizing to develop Darien. *Colono-campesino* land invasions, slash-and-burn agriculture, and uncontrolled cattle ranching are cutting into the forest. At the same time, indigenous Emberá-Wounaan communities are entering the 21st century cash economy, abandoning traditions that have allowed their coexistence in native ecosystems, and adopting unsustainable agricultural practices.

map courtesy of PRISMA

To meet these challenges, we are creating economic incentives that encourage forest preservation and improve access to education. These initiatives meet human needs and protect the rich biodiversity of Darien. For example, **soon we will expand and improve shade-grown coffee and cacao plantations to support jobs that don't harm the rain forest.** We already assist with chicken coops and plant nurseries to provide food and discourage the hunting of bush meat.

David L Anderson

We pioneered community-based conservation nearly thirty years ago in Madagascar, also a biodiversity hotspot. So far, we have helped 11 communities there organize to manage local resources, expanded the country's national protected areas by more than a million acres, and supported the education of hundreds of people as conservation leaders. Our experience of "saving raptors, enriching lives" at various scales around the world gives us high expectations for Darien.

Above: Transported to Belize by private charter, four fledgling captive-bred Orange-breasted Falcons are placed in a hack box, cared for by attendants and a resident pair of adult falcons prior to independence in the fall.

Right: 2010 released captive-bred male B1, superstar of The Peregrine Fund's restoration project in Belize, attracted a wild mate at the hack site and produced seven young before disappearing in 2017. He was replaced by his son P29.

Robert Berry

Always rare and widespread because of its specialized habitat requirements, the Orange-breasted Falcon now occupies only four percent of its historical range in Central America, limited to the Maya Mountains of Belize and along the Mirador Cordillera in Guatemala. Our surveys disclose that despite large areas of apparently suitable habitat, this falcon's numbers are in steep decline with fewer than 20 territorial pairs remaining now isolated by 1500 km from a few pairs in the Darien of Panama and the little-known population in South America.

If current trends continue, extinction of the remaining Central American population may occur in less than a decade. As the only captive breeder of Orange-breasted Falcons, we are poised...

THE PEREGRINE FUND

Above: Adult female named Caya (B1's mate) feeds her captive-bred foster child along with her own progeny (note tiny radio transmitter).

Our Impact:

In 2017 we surveyed 26 (10 by helicopter) of the 32 historic territories in Belize and Guatemala. Thirteen were occupied, and five fledged a total of 11 young.

One occupied territory—an artifical nest box at our hack site—is now populated by P29 (B1's son) and 047 from Tikal Park, 55 miles distant, highlighting the paucity of recruitable adult falcons.

We have released 50 captive-bred Orange-breasted Falcons with Panama origins since 2007 to bolster the small population and add diversity. They are surviving and breeding with wild mates.

Our new widely-distributed poster, along with educational programs focused on school children and their parents, seeks to change the culture away from viewing raptors as vermin and end persecution of all raptors in Belize.

1/2018

Orange-breasted Falcons appear to have unique survival advantages: they nest on towering cliffs in rugged and remote mountain habitat that they occupy year round. They care for their young three times as long as other falcon species. They have long reproductive lives of 10 or more years, similar to other falcon species, and yet our recent banding studies indicate that **the life expectancy of an adult Orange-breasted Falcon is just 2.57 years.**

We believe the cumulative effects of habitat alteration, fragmentation, human conflicts, and natural predation together help explain the large diminution in the species' range and continuing local decline. We can confirm that this once mountain species now leaves the sanctuary of its mountain home to hunt invasive feral pigeons and collared doves in the surrounding lowlands and cities, where all raptors are persecuted as vermin.

To help bolster this small declining northern population, each spring we conduct an arduous three-month long hack of captive-bred unrelated juveniles bred at our Wyoming facility—no small feat, since this species has proven to be the most difficult of falcon species to breed in captivity. Despite unforeseen high mortality, our captive-bred birds and their progeny are now breeding with wild mates, designed to increase genetic diversity, fitness, and future productivity.

DNA analysis of blood samples from the Orange-breasted Falcon's entire range is underway at the University of Wyoming, and we're partnering with Cornell's eBird to create models, map habitat, and help identify relatedness, population status, and guide future research.

We search for new pairs while monitoring known territories both on foot and by helicopter, including in the Darien region of Panama, a biodiversity "hotspot" where we also conserve Harpy Eagles. We plan to assist Darien's local communities to **create economic alternatives to forest destruction, benefiting raptors and numerous other species including the Orange-breasted Falcon.**

Russell Thorstrom

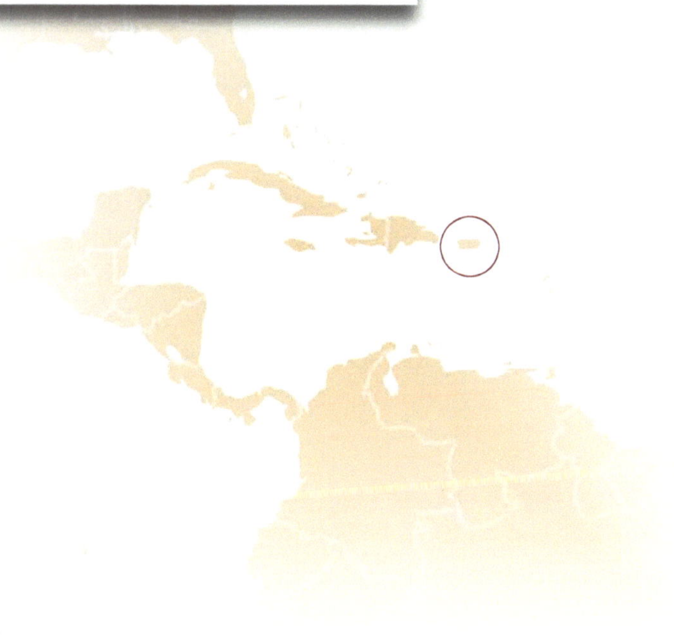

Even before Hurricanes Irma and Maria, the entire recorded population of Puerto Rican Sharp-shinned Hawks was just 75 individuals in the 2017 breeding season. We feared the worst after the hurricanes in September, wondering if any bird could survive sustained winds of 155 mph.

Sifting through the remains of the flattened forest in January, we found a small miracle: 19 Sharp-shinned Hawks survived. With few nest trees remaining and very little prey, we've mounted a rescue mission...

THE PEREGRINE FUND

Puerto Rican Sharp-shinned Hawks don't migrate, nor are they found anywhere beyond their island stronghold, in habitat depleted by human land use. The hawks depend entirely on the dense mountain forests of this Caribbean island for nesting and hunting. Like Sharp-shinned Hawks on the American mainlands, they are agile fliers, but they're smaller and have brighter plumage.

Of the 19 hardy survivors, nearly all are paired; but despite being well into the 2018 breeding season, only one pair is building a nest or showing signs of egg-laying. Their chance of success is extremely low. Hurricane Maria decimated the forests, actually stripping the leaves off the relatively few trees left standing. The majority of mature trees were blown down, uprooted, or snapped off, leaving only palm trees and tree ferns. Without foliage, any nestlings that might hatch won't be sheltered from heat, rain, or predators.

Russell Thorstrom

Even adult birds are subject to starvation because their main prey—small birds like tanagers, warblers, and vireos—also depend on adequate forest habitat. In such difficult conditions, it's unlikely that any of the remaining Sharp-shinned Hawks are healthy enough to breed successfully.

Our first step will be providing supplemental food to prevent starvation and enable the surviving hawks to lay eggs. As eggs appear—hopefully this spring—we'll carefully move them into incubators to hatch in a secure, climate-controlled conservation breeding facility on the island. Since these hawks normally produce a second set of eggs if the first set is lost, we'll be able to raise chicks in the safety of our facility without compromising the wild parents' success. The young we raise, ideally 5–10 adult pairs, can produce future young for release as nearby forests are restored by local partners. Given the scale of devastation in Puerto Rico's forests, we estimate a full recovery could take up to 20 years.

Few organizations have the expertise or resources to respond to an emergency of this scope, but The Peregrine Fund has returned numerous raptor species from the brink. We expect to learn a great deal in Puerto Rico. This rescue operation will hone our skills for a future of extreme weather and ever more threatened island species.

Thomas Hayes

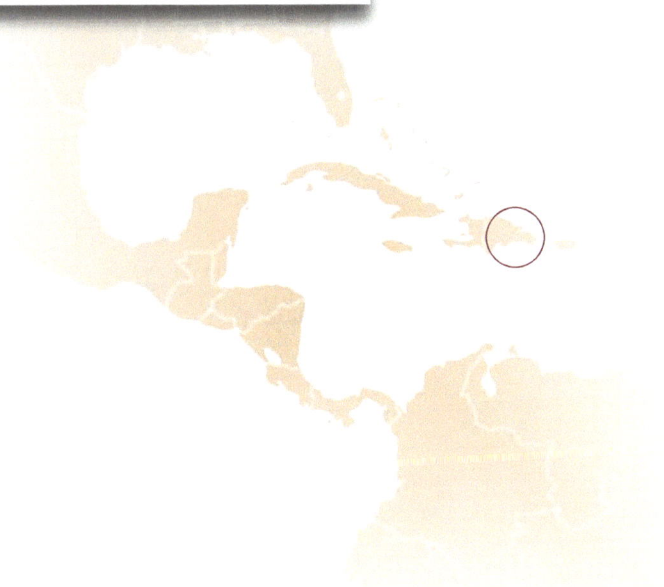

When The Peregrine Fund began investigating the Ridgway's Hawk, only about 300 remained. This charismatic species' habitat was lost to human development, restricting the remnant population to the small Los Haitises National Park on the northeastern coast of the Dominican Republic. A single forest fire, virus, or hurricane could have caused its extinction in the blink of an eye.

A closer look revealed a daunting collection of threats, requiring us to dig deeper than ever for creative solutions...

THE PEREGRINE FUND

CHANGE
to
THE
FUTURE

Our Impact:

In 2017 we recorded 123 pairs of Ridgway's Hawks raising 106 young in Los Haitises National Park. We relocated 25 young to Puntacana Resort. Since 2013, 22 wild-hatched young have fledged at Puntacana.

We trained six new volunteer field technicians, raising our local workforce to 23.

We reached more than 1,800 people through school presentations, teacher and youth training workshops, and door-to-door visits in 20 communities.

Over 100 people attended Ridgway's Hawk Day at the Santo Domingo Zoo, and over 70 students and teachers celebrated by visiting the Punta Cana release site.

Another 55 power poles have been retrofitted, for a total of 215 now adapted to prevent electrocutions.

We treated 68 nests for botfly parasites, resulting in more than four-fold greater success than for untreated nests!

1/2018

Habitat loss was just one of the many threats impacting Ridgway's Hawks. They were also being shot by people protecting their chickens. To make matters worse, botfly infestations frequently killed nestlings, resulting in reproductive rates that could barely sustain this fragile population.

This "perfect storm" of threats called for an equally perfect storm of innovation. We began by testing a technique called *assisted dispersal* to effectively "transplant" young hawks to new, safer territory and expand the species' range. At the same time, we informed residents in both areas that the hawks typically eat reptiles and small rodents — not chickens — and offered free cages to protect young poultry from all predators. Our school visits, printed field guides, and media interviews are changing attitudes towards Ridgway's Hawks and other raptors. We also hire and train residents as field technicians, and purchase locally-made handicrafts to offer in our gift shop, effectively stimulating the local economy while showing how conservation benefits birds *and* people.

Marta Curti

Once we knew assisted dispersal could work, we discovered a new problem: electrocution by power lines. We quickly partnered with the local utility company to retrofit power poles surrounding the new territory at Puntacana Resort and Club, where our "transplanted" population now thrives. The Grupo Puntacana Foundation promotes ecotourism and conservation programs, directly benefiting hawks.

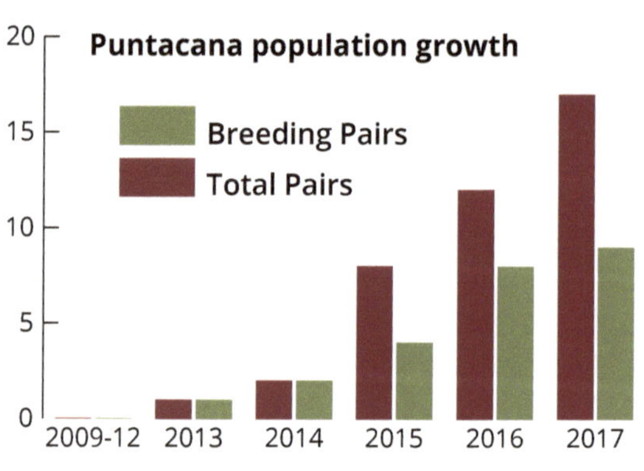

Botfly infestation is a more complex problem, but at nests where we applied a pesticide, **nestling survival rates increased more than four-fold.** This intervention is crucial for restoring the Ridgway's Hawk population while our researchers look for the causes of this ecological imbalance. Botflies are an emerging threat to species throughout the Caribbean, and our discoveries now will contribute to future conservation needs.

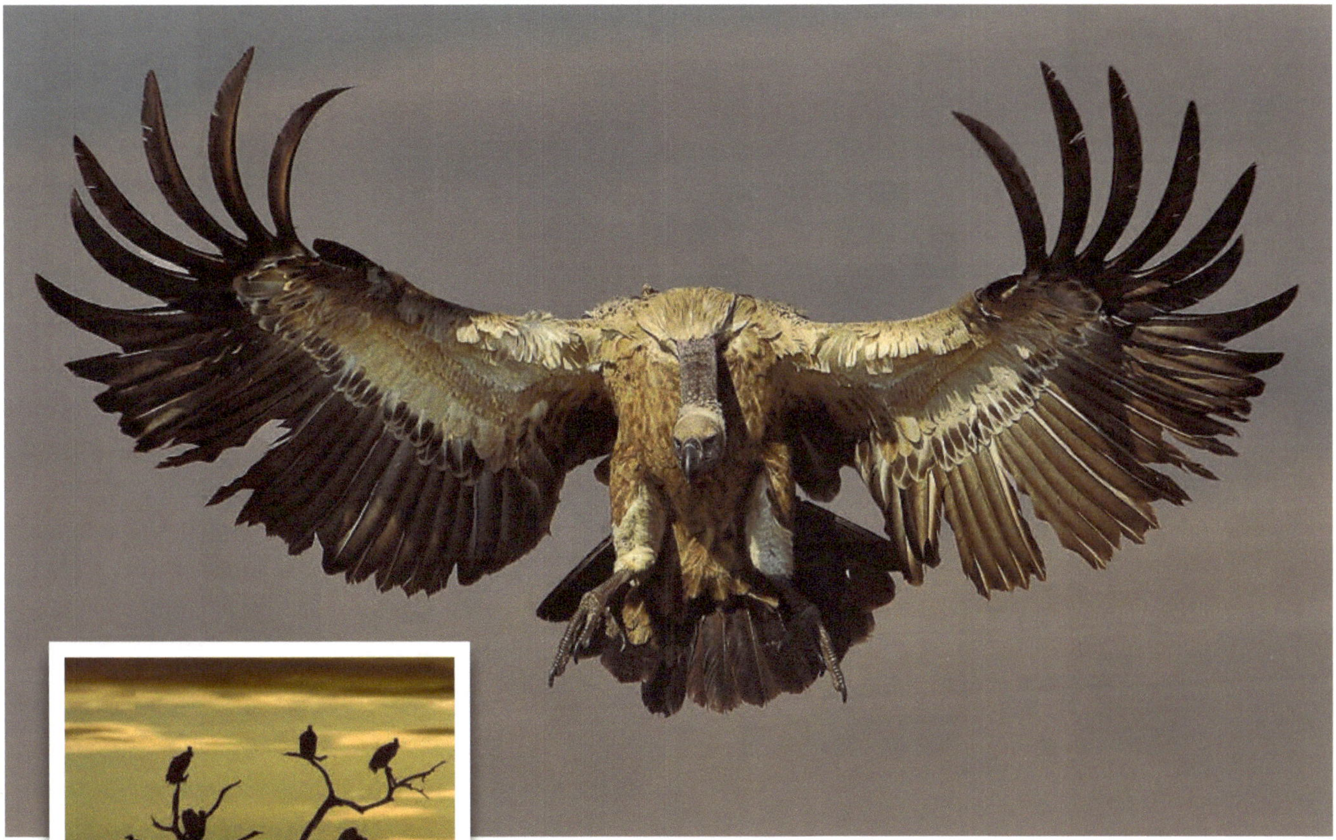

Percy Mitchell, ooaphotography.co.za

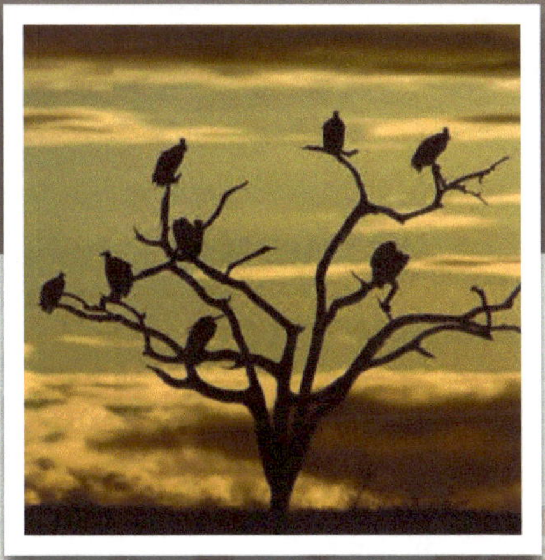

Munir Virani

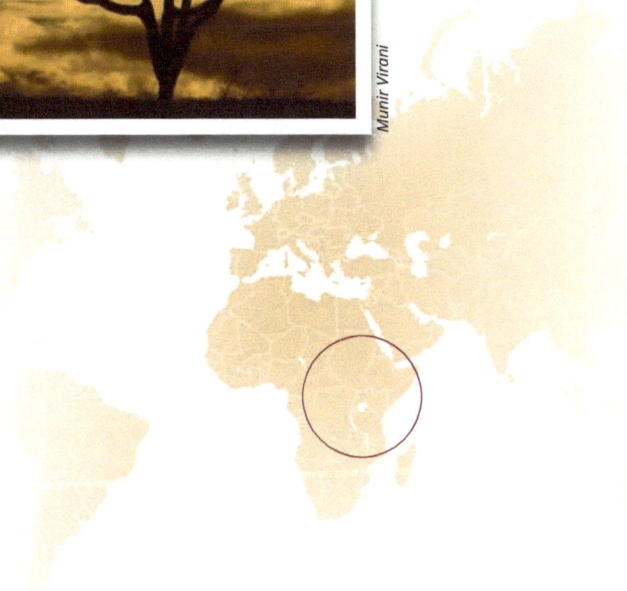

More than any other continent, Africa is known for a circle of life revolving around massive herds of migrating animals hunted by fierce predators. Vultures are critical to that circle as efficient "eco-janitors." Without them, diseases like rabies go unchecked, and the price is high—as demonstrated by a surge in human rabies deaths since south Asia's vulture populations began to crash in the 1990s.

Vulture numbers across Africa have plummeted for more than a decade. Against a backdrop of development, poaching, and poisoning incidents, we are racing...

As demand for power, food, and material goods escalates throughout Africa, The Peregrine Fund has risen to meet new threats to vultures. Chief among them is wildlife poisoning. Livestock owners use poison to target predators like lions and hyenas, inadvertently killing vultures and other scavengers. Poachers deliberately kill vultures to avoid having their crime scene exposed by circling birds.

In 2017 we began *Stop Poisonings Now: Empower, React, Deter*—a campaign to reduce poisoning at the grassroots level. Trainees learn to prevent the spread of poison from an incident, recover evidence, report to authorities, and raise awareness. They inform us of new poisoning methods and incidents, so we can tailor future responses and understand why people use poison. One of our trainees even saved a girl's life when poison was used to attempt suicide.

We have collected poisoning data since 2005 and share it in the African Wildlife Poisoning Database, which has recorded 272 poisoning incidents in 15 countries, and the deaths of more than 8,000 animals of 40 different species. **However grim, this data-gathering is the crucial spark for funding and action.**

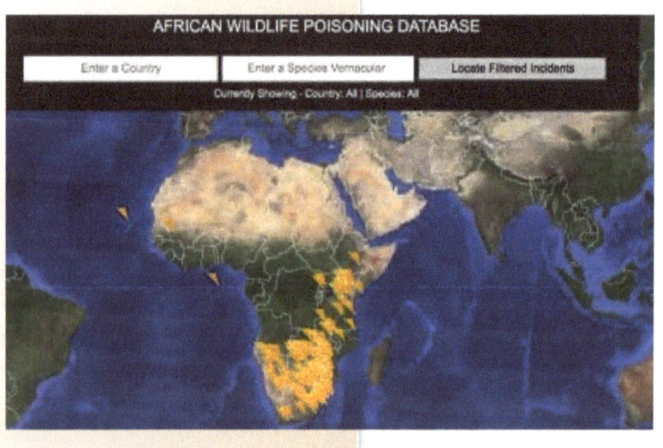

Darcy Ogada

We tag and track vultures (left) to understand their movements. Not only can we learn where vultures are most likely to encounter poison, but our data are also valuable to energy developers in proper siting of new wind farms. Vultures are one of the few bird species for which tracking data is available in Kenya, giving conservation a credible voice on this rapidly-changing continent.

Another outstanding example of data-driven results is the African Raptor Databank (ARDB), a smartphone app used by biologists to record raptor sightings. Using ARDB, partners helped us document declines of up to 80% in eight African vulture species, justifying their uplisting to Endangered or Critically Endangered. **The status upgrades sounded the alarm internationally, prompting multiple organizations to redirect funds and staff.** The shared databank concept is so powerful that we expanded it to our new Global Raptor Impact Network so we can assess all 586 raptor species worldwide.

Lily-Arison Rene de Roland

Islands are some of the most richly-diverse places on Earth, home to life evolved in isolated, unique habitats. Madagascar, the world's fourth-largest island, boasts 310 bird species in an area the size of Montana and Idaho combined. More than half of those species are found nowhere else.

The Peregrine Fund went to Madagascar in 1990 to search out rare, endangered birds of prey, and we found them—even some that were thought to be extinct. **To conserve those species, we had to devise radical new ways of empowering local people...**

THE PEREGRINE FUND

CHANGE the FUTURE

Like its neighboring island of Mauritius, where we had helped restore the Mauritius Kestrel from just four survivors, Madagascar had a wealth of diversity but little infrastructure for understanding or protecting it. Of the 24 raptor species on the island, 14 are endemic—found nowhere else—and of these, two had not been seen for more than 60 years. Our biologists re-discovered both, plus a missing duck species, and even found four previously unknown lemur species!

Discoveries are thrilling, but preserving species in perpetuity is a complex undertaking. Habitat alone is not enough; human pressures call for human vigilance, and **this realization, reinforced by our success, resulted in a rapid paradigm shift for conservation worldwide.**

Our early insights came from people living near degraded wetlands where we found Madagascar Fish Eagles struggling to survive. Sustainable village traditions

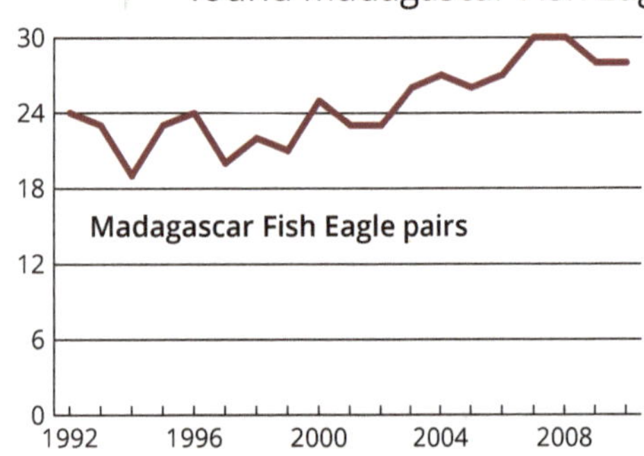

were being violated by newcomers, and residents could protect neither their own livelihoods nor the wildlife. **We helped form the first local association in Madagascar with legal authority to enforce limits on resource use.** Under a new federal law, the community was empowered, the eagle population stabilized, and today those wetlands are a pristine habitat supporting wildlife and people.

Lily-Arison Rene de Roland

Working with local associations keeps raptor conservation at the forefront. For example, we supply fiberglass canoes so that fishermen no longer make dugout canoes from mature trees, preserving choice nest sites. We distribute special fishing nets, reducing the use of nets that ensnare and kill fish eagles. Reforestation projects provide food for people and habitat for wildlife. Community wells, hydroelectric power, eco-tourism, honey production, and schools are all made possible by our simple philosophy of "saving raptors, enriching lives."

We now work with 11 local associations close to our raptor conservation sites, and the benefits reach beyond individual villages; **together, we have added almost a half million acres of habitat to the country's National Protected Areas**—equal in size to Great Smoky Mountain National Park in the United States.

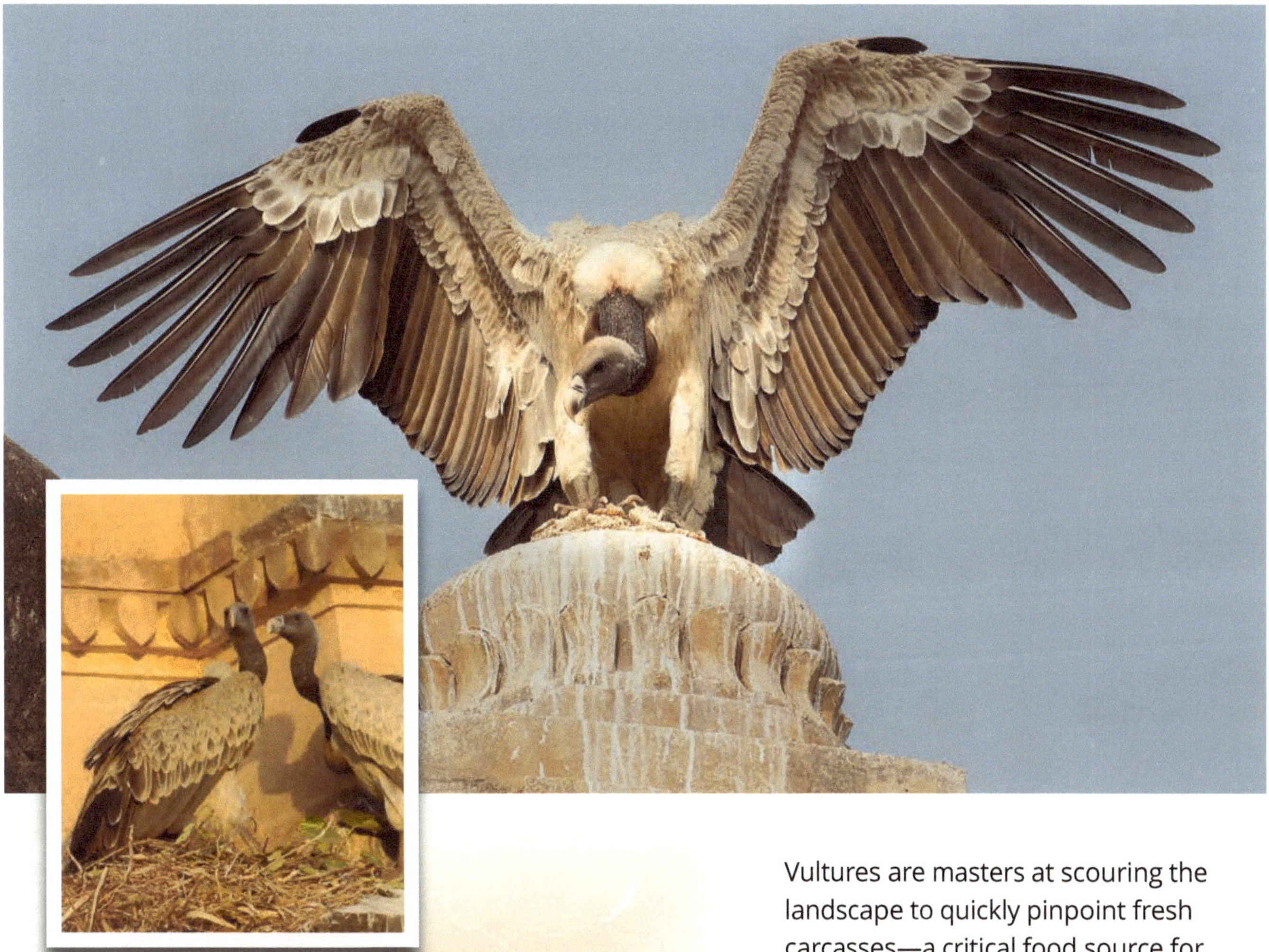

Munir Virani

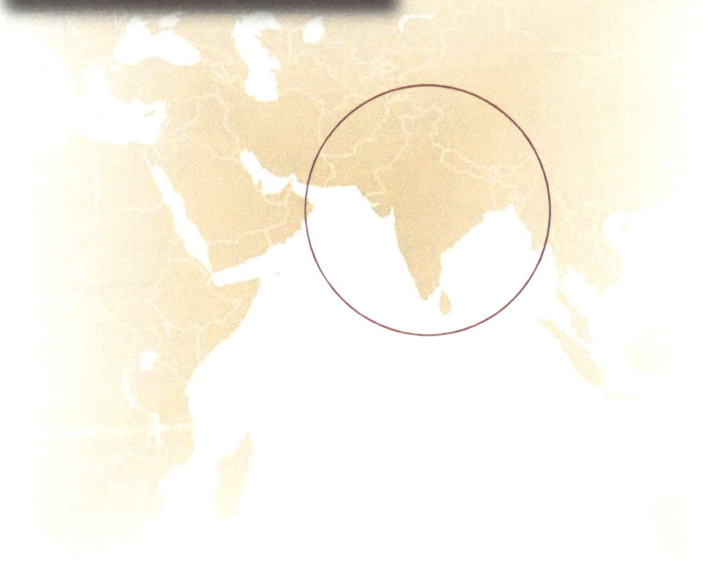

Vultures are masters at scouring the landscape to quickly pinpoint fresh carcasses—a critical food source for them, but a bacteria-laden hazard to humans. Vultures' adaptations—high stomach acidity, crushing bill strength, and featherless heads for staying clean—guarantee efficient clean-up, so disease-spreading scavengers like rats, feral dogs, and flies don't multiply.

From the mid-1990s, vulture populations throughout south Asia crashed with up to 99% of some species literally dropping dead without explanation. Finding the cause was grim, difficult work, but we persisted...

Our Impact:

Three vulture species in Asia were destined for extinction in less than a decade, a catastrophe unprecedented since the loss of billions of passenger pigeons in the last century. Peregrine Fund biologists struggled to understand how tens of millions could die so rapidly, and through meticulous forensic investigations discovered the answer in 2003: an inexpensive, readily-available drug called diclofenac sodium had been introduced in the region for treating sick cattle. Consuming even small traces of diclofenac in cattle remains causes rapid kidney failure in vultures. Since only four percent of an estimated 500 million cattle in India are for human consumption, the availability of carrion for scavengers is significant.

The Peregrine Fund advocated along with conservation and government partners to ban veterinary use of diclofenac in Nepal, Pakistan, and India, and bans

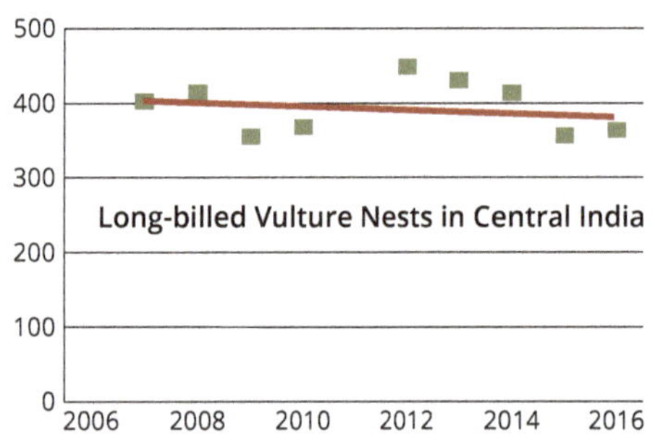

were enacted three years later. To measure the bans' effects, we monitor 450 pairs of Long-billed Vultures in the Indian states of Madhya Pradesh and Rajasthan. The population stabilized in the five-year period after the ban was enacted, leading us to believe a positive trend had begun; but **more recently we've observed declines, pointing to a need for vigilance and further action.**

Munir Virani

Diclofenac is still available for humans, and can easily be misused for treating livestock. At least seven other veterinary drugs on the market are potentially toxic to vultures, and new drugs may appear without thorough testing. We work closely with partners in south Asia who are identifying vulture-safe alternatives and encouraging tighter regulation of toxic veterinary drugs. We also track 13 Bearded Vultures (photo above) to study their habits and territories, and we support graduate students throughout south Asia to increase our capacity to deal with future crises.

In 2017, the **United Nations Convention on Migratory Species** recognized The Peregrine Fund in a Raptors Memorandum of Understanding. The Convention seeks to halt population declines of 15 vulture species across Africa and Eurasia and recommends 124 actions for countries to restore numbers by 2029.

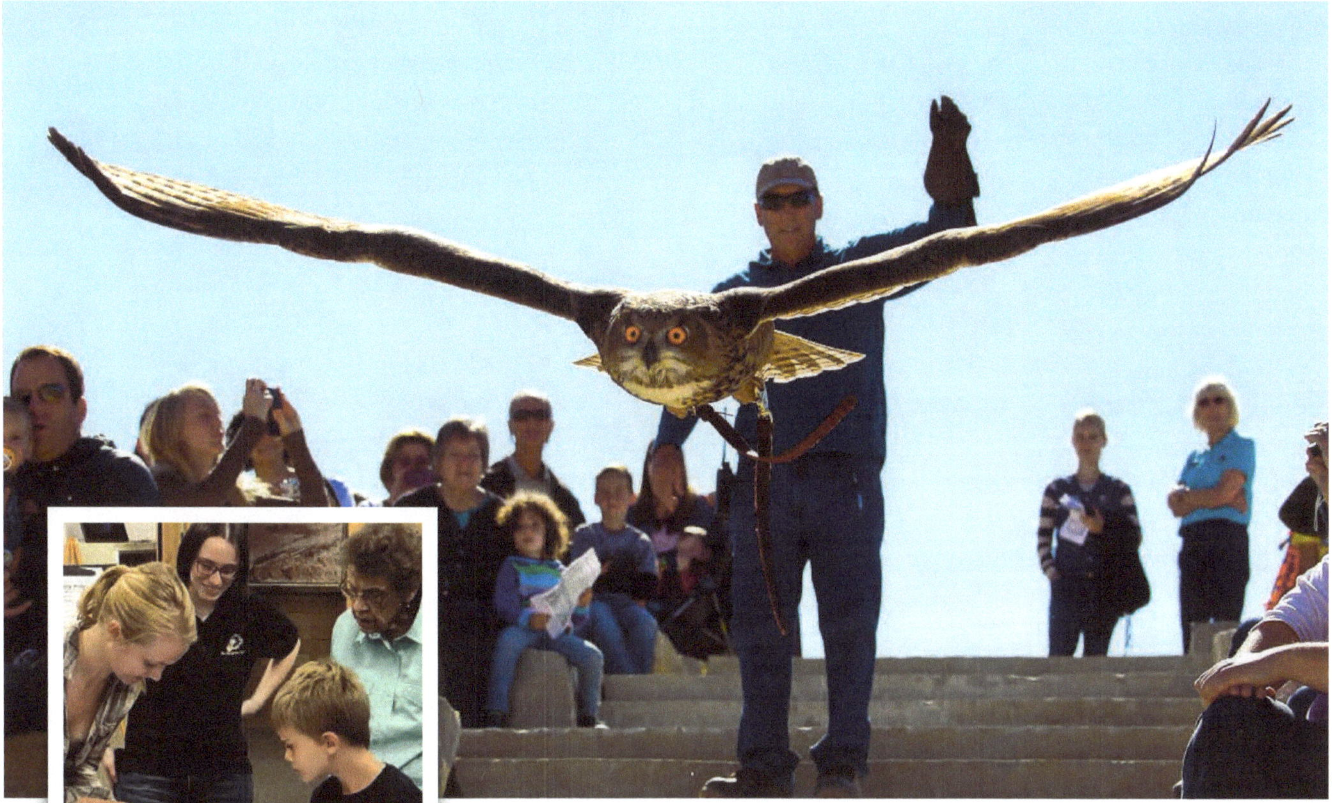

Jeffrey L. Armstrong

Erin Katzner

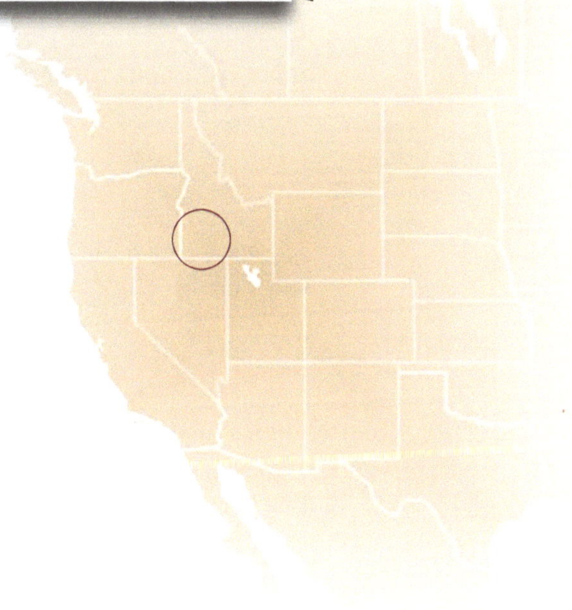

The World Center for Birds of Prey is the heartbeat of The Peregrine Fund's education program. Situated in one of the most densely populated raptor regions in the world, it is an international destination for 50,000+ people a year. Visitors experience raptors up close and personally through live, daily raptor demonstrations and interactions with staff, volunteers, and exhibits that create a deeper understanding of these incredible birds and our role in conserving them for future generations.

We're influencing people's attitudes, emotions, knowledge, and behaviors about raptors and wild places....

THE PEREGRINE FUND

The Peregrine Fund's vision is to create a world where birds of prey are valued by all humans. Our Visitor Center serves as the foundation for empowering guests to save raptors and find solutions that protect wild places we all need for survival.

At the World Center for Birds of Prey, visitors come nose-to-beak with raptors from around the world while learning about conservation work The Peregrine Fund leads on a global scale to save each species. When people have the opportunity to experience one of our avian ambassadors up close, an emotional connection can form that changes attitudes toward conservation in a positive way.

The recovery story of the Peregrine Falcon is one of the greatest conservation success stories of all time. It is a story of people coming together to tackle an environmental problem that affects us all. **The message is clear— we have the power to save species when we work together.** The World Center for Birds of Prey has shared this empowering message with nearly one million visitors since opening our doors in 1994.

As we approach our 50th anniversary in 2020, The Peregrine Fund has renewed our commitment to education and public engagement. The World Center for Birds of Prey is expanding our footprint to showcase our international conservation work in partnership with local communities and increase exposure to native raptors and conservation efforts that promote coexistence between humans and the natural world, with wise stewardship of the land.

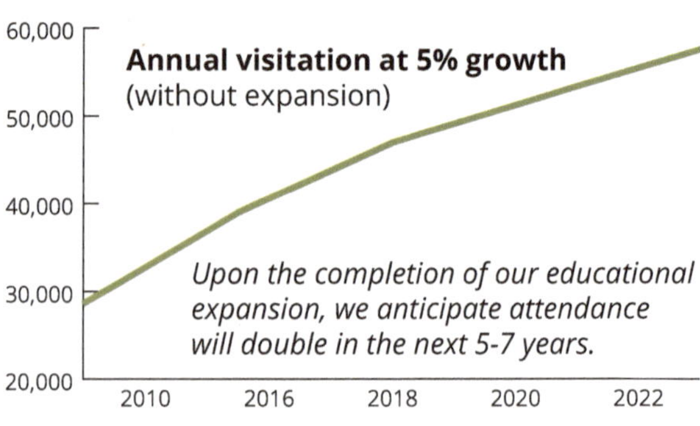

To learn more about our educational expansion, please contact Heather Meuleman, Campaign Director, at *hmeuleman@peregrinefund.org* or 208.362-2840.

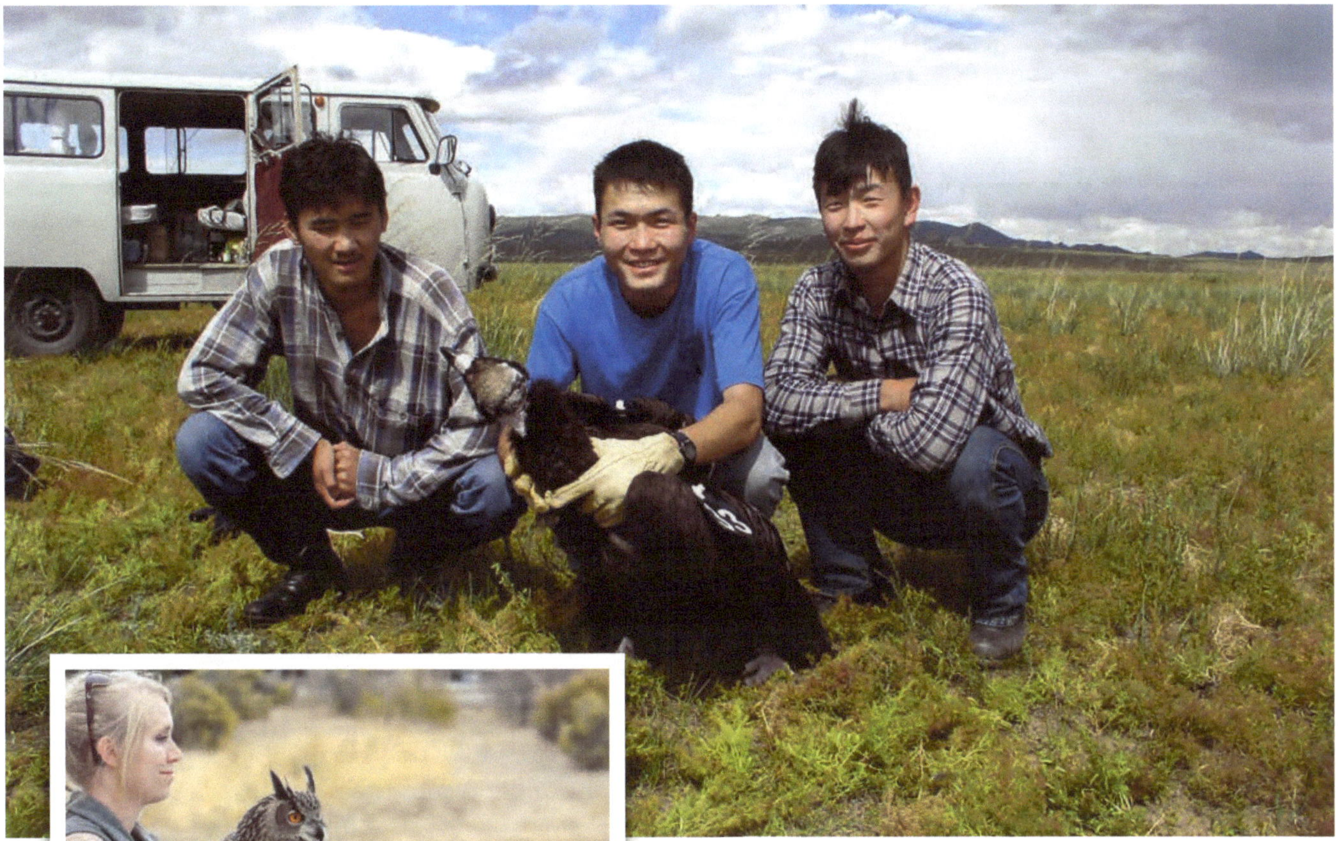

Nyambayar Batbayar

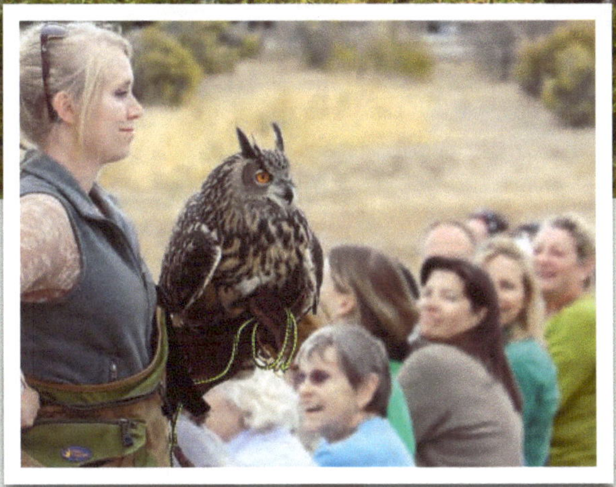

Paul Spurling

More than half of all raptor species worldwide are in decline, and the causes almost always point to rapid growth of human populations. To prevent extinction, it's more urgent than ever to inspire, teach, and connect with people of all ages, in every corner of the globe. The fate of raptor species is in their hands.

People value birds of prey and want to protect them, but they need The Peregrine Fund as a catalyst, empowering them...

THE PEREGRINE FUND

As our scientists have traveled to the far reaches of the globe, we have made important discoveries about birds of prey; but **equally important are fresh insights into human behavior.** We know, for example, that people are intensely curious and sometimes shoot raptors to get a closer look. We have learned that people who come to understand a raptor's role and life history will gladly make accommodations that allow them to thrive. And finally, we've found that when raptors are part of a holistic picture that includes economic incentives — like local jobs, ecotourism, education, or sustainable food — people become champions for birds of prey.

Donatien Randrianjafiniasa

Truly empowering people challenges us to reach out in meaningful ways… and **with 586 raptor species and billions of people on the planet, our outreach must take many forms.** Face-to-face and "nose-to-beak" interactions are ideal, so whenever possible we let raptors speak for themselves in classrooms and communities near our projects and at our visitor center in Boise, Idaho. When personal contact isn't possible, we count on video, photography, and vivid storytelling to connect people with birds of prey.

Sometimes our outreach doesn't involve a bird at all; instead we provide basic needs like fishing nets, chicken coops, tree seedlings, career training, tuition, and connections to government resources. We call this approach "saving raptors, enriching lives," because it offers a way to make room for raptors by improving opportunities for people, their communities, and the next generation.

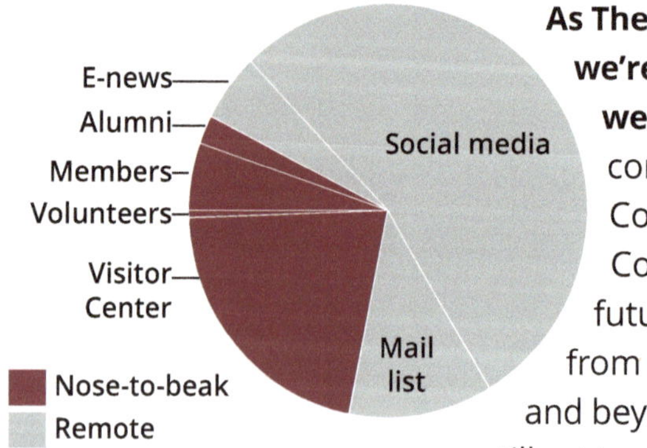

As The Peregrine Fund nears its 50th year, we're reflecting on the millions of lives we've already touched along the path to conserving Peregrine Falcons, California Condors, and hundreds of other species. Confident that we can again change the future, we're calling on all of our "alumni," from members to students to birdwatchers and beyond, to support raptors while we can still act to prevent extinction.

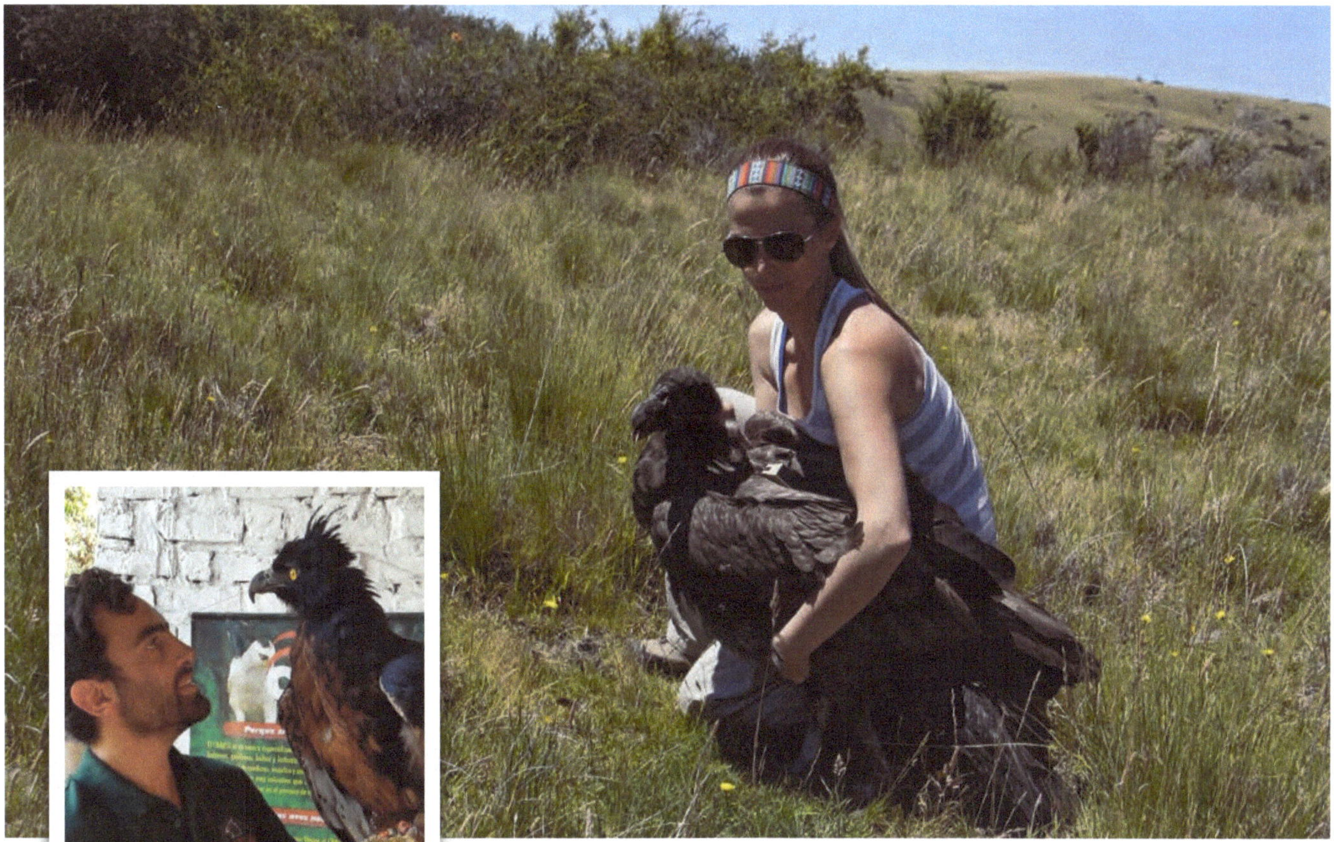

Gonzalo Ignasi

Alex Ospina

Studying raptors requires a rare set of traits: an obsession with birds, the grit to find and document them in rugged conditions, and the discipline to analyze and publish credible results.

Because conservation hinges on scientific rigor, we seek out and encourage the kind of peer-reviewed, published work taught by universities—but that level of education is not easily accessible to everyone. **Exceptional students around the world need our support in becoming scientists and leaders...**

THE PEREGRINE FUND

Higher education is at the very root of The Peregrine Fund; in fact, Cornell University was our first home, established in a breeding barn by Professor Tom Cade when he joined the faculty there in 1970. Academic rigor informs every one of our strategies, and like all teachers **we look for opportunities to nurture students' curiosity, resourcefulness, and connection to a global community.**

Our projects provide invaluable experience for motivated students. In Pakistan, student Jamshed Chaudry has witnessed first-hand the catastrophic decline of the region's vulture species and participated in the recovery efforts. In Kenya, Washington Wachira studied Crowned Eagles and spoke at the prestigious TED

Global Platform (left) on his love of birds. In Argentina, Amira Salom based her thesis on interviews with local people about their perceptions of birds of prey.

With our guidance, students turn field experiences into career-changing results: Dr. Lily-Arison René de Roland was our very first master's-level student in Madagascar and has since completed doctorate and post-doctorate work, received recognition as a Disney Conservation Hero, and serves now as National Director of our Madagascar project. Dr. Hernan Vargas, director of our Neotropical Science and Student Education program, started with limited opportunities in the Galapagos Islands and got his "big break" with a Peregrine Fund grant to study raptor biology at Boise State University. He now directs the studies of dozens of students throughout Central and South America. With our support, Nyamba Batbayar studied raptor biology at Boise State University and went home to found the Wildlife Science and Conservation Center of Mongolia.

Most students we assist go on to influential positions in their home countries, serving in wildlife management, government agencies, and other non-profits. As local residents, they can navigate cultural norms that might present obstacles to a foreigner. When conservation crises occur, these in-country partners are trained and ready to respond.

Our students are so valuable to the future of raptors that we've formalized our mentoring plans with **one audacious goal: to establish a raptor biologist in every country in the world.** We're focusing on Africa and South America because of their fast-growing economies and high demand for education. Threats to raptors and other biodiversity are rapidly increasing on both continents, meaning our students' impact is likely to be significant and long-lasting.

Office Locations

Headquarters
World Center for Birds of Prey
5668 West Flying Hawk Lane
Boise, ID 83709
United States of America

email: tpf@peregrinefund.org

Arizona Field Office
P.O. Box 6123
Marble Canyon, AZ 86036

Africa Field Office
P.O. Box 45111
Nairobi, Kenya 00100

Madagascar Field Office
B.P. 4113
Antananarivo (101)
Madagascar

South America Field Office
Casilla 17-17-1044
Quito
Ecuador

Board of Directors

Officers

Steven P. Thompson
Chairman of the Board

Carter R. Montgomery
Vice-Chairman
Central Energy Partners, LP

Richard T. Watson, Ph.D.
President and CEO

Patricia B. Manigault
Treasurer
Conservationist
and Rancher

Samuel Gary, Jr.
Secretary
President, Samuel Gary, Jr.
& Associates, Inc.

Tom J. Cade, Ph.D.
Founding Chairman
Professor Emeritus of
Ornithology, Cornell
University

Lee M. Bass
Chairman Emeritus
President, Lee M. Bass, Inc.

Carl E. Navarre
Chairman Emeritus
Investor

Ian Newton,
D.Phil., D.Sc., FRS.
Chairman Emeritus
Senior Ornithologist (RET)
Natural Environment
Research Council
United Kingdom

Directors

Robert B. Berry
Trustee, Wolf Creek
Charitable Foundation,
Rancher, Falcon Breeder,
and Conservationist

Harry L. Bettis
Rancher

P. Dee Boersma, Ph.D.
Wadsworth Endowed Chair
in Conservation Science
University of Washington

L. Michael Bogert
Attorney
Parsons Behle & Latimer

G. Kent Burnett
VP Technology and
E-commerce (RET)
Dillard's Inc.

Virginia H. Carter
Natural History Artist
Environmental Educator

Robert J. Collins
Curator
The Archives of Falconry

Robert S. Comstock
Fashion Designer
Robert Comstock Company

Scott A. Crozier
President
General Counsel Concierge

Ralph H. Duggins
Partner,
Cantey Hanger, LLP
Chairman, Texas Parks
and Wildlife Commission

Caroline A. Forgason
Partner
Groves-Alexander
Group LLC

Mark R. Fuller
Scientist Emeritus
US Geological Services

Victor L. Gonzalez
President
Windmar Renewable
Energy

H. Dale Hall
Chief Executive Officer
Ducks Unlimited, Inc.

Karen J. Hixon
Conservationist

Grainger Hunt
Senior Scientist
Emeritus (RET)
The Peregrine Fund

Jay L. Johnson
JLJ Consulting
Admiral, U.S. Navy (RET)

Carolynn D. Loacker
Vineyard Owner and
Philanthropist

Ambrose K. Monell
Private Investor

Calen B. Offield
Director, Offield Family
Foundation and
Photographer

Lucia Liu Severinghaus
Biodiversity Research
Center (RET)
Academia Sinica, Taiwan

Catherine A. Stevens
Attorney
Mayer-Brown

Dan Tomascheski
VP-Timber Resources
Sierra Pacific Industries

R. Beauregard Turner
Fish & Wildlife Manager,
Director of Natural
Resources
Turner Enterprises, Inc.

James D. Weaver
President, Grasslans
Charitable Foundation
and Rancher

Tim Wilcomb
Principal/President
Jordan-Wilcomb
Construction, Inc.

Financial Statement

The Peregrine Fund's complete audited financial statements may be viewed on our website, *www.peregrinefund.org* or a statement may be obtained by contacting The Peregrine Fund, Accounting, 5668 W Flying Hawk Lane, Boise, ID 83709.

Expenses

Conservation Programs (total): 87%

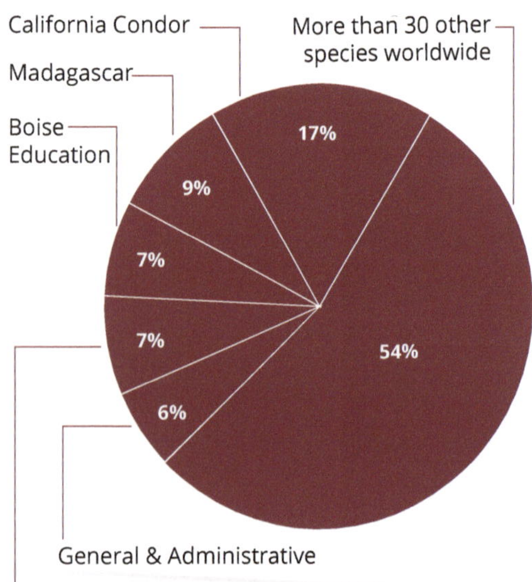

Revenues

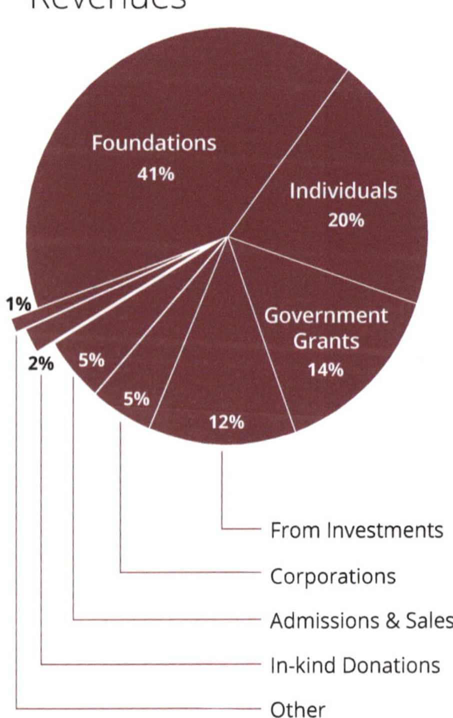

Statement of Activities FOR THE YEAR ENDED SEPTEMBER 30

UNRESTRICTED OPERATIONS

Revenues	2017	2016
Contributions utilized (note 1)	4,001,147	3,994,107
Government grants	773,238	794,338
In-kind revenues	81,063	82,295
Admissions and sales	255,140	226,077
Board designated funds utilized (from investments)	631,200	656,000
Other	31,703	25,629
Total unrestricted revenues, gains, and other support	**5,773,491**	**5,778,446**
Expenses		
PROGRAM EXPENSES	**5,202,931**	**4,962,737**
SUPPORT SERVICES EXPENSES		
Administration	351,623	585,474
Fundraising and Membership	457,227	506,629
Total support services expenses	**808,850**	**1,092,103**
Total expenses-operations	6,011,781	6,054,840
OPERATING REVENUES OVER EXPENSES	**(238,290)**	**(276,394)**

NON-OPERATING ACTIVITIES

Capital		
Contributions utilized to purchase fixed assets	147,187	200,737
Depreciation on Fixed Assets	(254,436)	(300,073)
Gain on asset disposition	6,062	3,500
Endowment/Board Designated Funds		
Board designated - bequests and in memorium	94,062	1,028,680
Investment income (loss)	1,760,610	1,391,917
Board designated funds utilized (from investments)	(631,200)	(656,000)
Pledges and contributions designated for future years		
Pledges and contributions	271,740	1,104,834
Prior year's revenue used in current year	(877,704)	(178,121)
TOTAL NON-OPERATING ACTIVITIES	**516,321**	**2,595,474**
Increase (decrease) in net assets	**278,031**	**2,319,080**
Net assets at beginning of year	**22,462,433**	**20,143,353**
Net assets at end of year	**22,740,464**	**22,462,433**

Note 1 - Contributions utilized in 2017 includes current year contributions of $3,123,443 and prior years' contributions released from restrictions of $877,704

Statement of Financial Position AT SEPTEMBER 30

Assets	2017	2016
Cash and cash equivalents	522,528	860,123
Grants receivable	167,358	62,433
Promises to give and other receivables	275,980	977,146
Inventory, prepaids, and other assets	119,480	132,621
Property and equipment (net of depreciation)	3,975,133	4,076,320
Archives collection	2,648,952	2,648,952
Investments, Endowment and board designated	15,266,539	14,057,127
TOTAL ASSETS	**22,975,970**	**22,814,722**

Liabilities and Net Assets	2017	2016
LIABILITIES		
Accounts payable	91,737	72,039
Accrued payroll and taxes	143,769	269,325
Deferred Revenue	-	10,925
TOTAL LIABILITIES	**235,506**	**352,289**
NET ASSETS		
Unrestricted	21,413,308	20,493,798
Temporarily restricted	1,227,156	1,868,635
Permanently Restricted	100,000	100,000
TOTAL NET ASSETS	**22,740,464**	**22,462,433**
TOTAL LIABILITIES AND NET ASSETS	**22,975,970**	**22,814,722**

Rick Ashworth & Dawn Roy
Edward G. Bourne
Karen D. Brender
Dorothy A. Clifford
Frank T. Curtin
Marie A. DeAngelis
Cynthia Ferguson
Esther Garnsey
Edward F. Gerrity
Gerald & Kathryn Herrick
Denise Kodner
Karl & Linda Kuivinen
Irmgard M. Light
Don McCartney
Beverly Miller
Velma V. Morrison
Theodore & Madeleine Noehren
Thomas K. Oliver
Gertrude Oschwald
Margaret W. Owings
Peter G. Pfendler
Joseph J. Pisar
Edward M. Roberts
Edward W. Rose, III
Dr. Stella M. Schmittner
Beth B. Seymour
Mary Blackmon Smith
Marie J. Vance
Christian W Westphal
Jim Willmarth
Erica B. Woodman
Gloria M. Young

Almost 50 years ago, our founders resolved to save Peregrine Falcons from extinction. Their life's work is a legacy we all enjoy each time we glimpse one of these magnificent birds in the wild.

The Peregrine Fund's planned giving society

You, too, can give the gift of raptor conservation by including The Peregrine Fund in your estate plans. You will join a special group of donors who receive permanent recognition at the World Center for Birds of Prey in Boise, invitations to special events, and recognition in the annual report (unless you wish to be anonymous).

Your bequest, annuity, or other planned gift further strengthens the foundation of all our conservation work, giving future generations the tools they'll need for a changing world.

Please let us know when you include The Peregrine Fund in your plans. Use the form at *www.peregrinefund.org/legacy-circle*, e-mail us at *legacycircle@peregrinefund.org* or call 406–388-7717.

Members and donors are the lifeblood of The Peregrine Fund, and we respect and appreciate everyone who contributes to our mission. To protect your privacy, we are not publishing a general membership list in our annual report.

We welcome your calls and emails if you have questions about your membership. Linda Behrman, our Director of Membership, is available at **208-362-3716 or lbehrman@peregrinefund.org.**

The Peregrine Fund

www.peregrinefund.org • 208|362-3716

Leadership Council members remain crucial to our success by giving $1,000 or more annually. In addition to regular member benefits, they receive a personalized desktop paperweight, invitations to board meetings and special events, an annual conference call with the President, one Gift Membership to give, a behind-the-scenes tour at the World Center for Birds of Prey, quarterly updates from the President, and recognition in the annual report. Learn more at **www.peregrinefund.org/leadership-council.**

David Anderson

Roger and Lora Anderson

Chester and Theresa Andrew

Mrs. Lucinda Attaway

A.J. and Susie Balukoff

Carter Bates

Max W. Batzer

Mrs. Margaret M. Betchart

Dr. Richard Bierregaard and Ms. Cathy Dolan

Dr. P. Dee Boersma

Cecilia Brown

Perry and Marilyn Brown

Kelly Browne

Dr. and Mrs. Tom J. Cade

Clay Cannady

Janet Chisman

Tom Connors

Donald and Michelle Cronin

Scott and Mary Crozier

Ms. Heather Cunningham and Mr. Doug Bullock

Count Charles de Ganay

Noah Drever

Tom and Jodi Duckett

Ralph H. Duggins

Jeremy Eddie

Paul and Janet Edie

Devon and Katherine Elstun

Morris and Wendy Evans

Leo E. Faddis

Kristine Floyd

Paul and Susie Frank

Rebecca Gaples and Simon Harrison

Mr. and Mrs. Victor Luis Gonzalez

Barbara Grace

Mr. and Mrs. Z. Wayne Griffin, Jr.

Helen K. Groves

Richard and Sondra Hackborn

Rhonda Hairford

Dr. Kathryn Ann Hale

Mr. and Mrs. Frederic C. Hamilton, Jr.

Dick and Barbara Harley

Jeff Hatch

Linda Helding

Dr. Stephen Hill

Barney and Anne Holland

The Horizon Foundation

Jillian and Po Huang

Michael and Candace Humphreys

Shirley F. Hunt

Kirk and Debra Hunter

J. Peter and Barbara Jenny

Admiral and Mrs. Jay L. Johnson

Donald and Mary Kayser

Steve and Paula Kehoe

Lisa Kern and Nancy Caspersen

Luther King Capital Management

Harvey and Mary King

Luther and Teresa King

Loraine E. Klinger

Brian and Terrie Knox

Cynthia Knox

Jeffrey Kolb

Susan LaFontaine

Mike and Jayme Lahey

Gary Landers

William Lazar

John S. Mackiewicz, Ph.D.

Diann MacRae

Paul and Linda Mascuch

Theresa Massey

Don and Kay McCarter

Mr. and Mrs. Don McCartney

Mrs. Paul L. Miller

Ambrose and Lili Monell

Nikolaos Monoyios and Valerie Brackett

Kellie J. Morrison

Sandra J. Moss

Dr. Margery A. Nicolson

Jim Norton

Donald and Cathy Ormond

Nathaniel O. Owings

Elizabeth B. Parks

Michael Peleg

Sheila and Ron Pera

Dr. Michael Pilch

Dr. Marshall F. Priest

Joel Rea

Mark Rockefeller

Allison Rohnert

Robert and Marcia Ross

Joseph and Alice Lee Ruf

Mr. and Mrs. Johnny Russell

Cynthia S. Schotte

Richard T. Schotte

Kyle Shannon

Marion Simpson

Jennifer P. Speers

Peter Spiegelman

Sheila Spiwak

Julie Kelleher Stacy

Catherine G. Symchych

Mr. Robert W. Tafel, Jrl and Mrs. Susan M. Tafel

Troy and Carrie Taylor

Joe and Flinda Terteling

Mr. and Mrs. Steve Thompson

David Thomson

Peter T. Toot

Dr. Ann Truesdale

J.T. "Skip" Tubbs

Christie Van Cleve

Judith VanTill

William and Noel Wade, Jr.

Joe and Judi Wagner

Judy Weidner and Wayne Richard

Kathryn and Gregory Weyland

Melanie Wirtanen

Carol A. Wolf

In Memory

Gifts were given to The Peregrine Fund in memory of the following in 2017:

Kelly R. Baxter

Daniel Berger

Frank M. Bond

Daniel J. Brimm

Pat Brown

Sterling Bunnell

Constance Burgess

Dr. Bill Burnham

Esther F. Butler

Paul A. Clark

Brian A. Craft

John Craighead

Ronald M. Crawford

LaVonne Cropley

Peggy Dean

Paul DeBenedictis

Richard J. Donnelly

Linda Edson

Phil Eldredge

Ron Elmone

James H. Enderson

Norval C. Fairman

Larry Fallstrom

Marjorie K. Fee

Kathryn Fraser

Spike Funk

Richard Fyfe

Therese M. Genne

Virginia Hageman

Charles Hamel

Christina M. Hasel

Donald W. Heidt

Dylan Hopkins

Dan Horn

Stephen Emery Tarcisius Kacir

Alicia S. Kromas

Vera Leach

Londa Lehman

Kublai Losee

Tom Maechtle

Lillie Mastin

Robert McCallum

Bob McCullum

Heinz Meng

Ken Mesch

Clay Miller

Rima Miller

Robert Minton

Rande Money

Ian Kay Muir

Marie I. Naidis

Morlan W. Nelson

R. W. Nelson

John Noble

Jack C. Osgood

Floyd Presley

Susan B. Preston

Gary A. Rickard

Ilene Robbins

Michael Roche

Dolores M. Rollins

James E. Sailer

Thomas Scheib

Charles Schwartz

Sharpshin hit by my truck

Marilyn T. Shuler

Bill Simons

Michael C. Smith

Wilbur F. Snelling

Robert M. Stabler

Kenneth Sterner

John E. Stieglitz

Russ Taylor

Colton Thorstrom-Smith

Denis R. Trowbridge

Jeff Turner

David Voss

Winifred Washco

Barrie D. Watson

Peter Watzke

John West

Dallas V. Willey

Lawrence E. Zuk